A Map of

MEXICO CITY BLUES

Jack Kerouac as Poet

James T. Jones

Southern Illinois University Press
Carbondale and Edwardsville

Grateful acknowledgment is made to quote excerpts from Jack Kerouac,
Mexico City Blues, published by Grove Press, 1959.

Library of Congress Cataloging-in-Publication Data

Jones, James T., 1948–
    A map of Mexico City blues : Jack Kerouac as poet / James T.
Jones.
        p. cm.
    Includes bibliographical references and indexes.
    1. Kerouac, Jack, 1922–1969. Mexico City blues. 2. Kerouac,
Jack, 1922–1969—Poetic works. 3. Mexico in literature. I. Title.
    PS3521.E735M435 1992 1993
    811'.54—dc20   91-40769
    ISBN 0-8093-1828-8   CIP

73428

For Allen Ginsberg and Anne Waldman,
cofounders of the Jack Kerouac School
of Disembodied Poetics

In him those holy antique hours are seen,
Without all ornament, itself and true,
Making no summer of another's green,
Robbing no old to dress his beauty new.
    And him as for a map doth Nature store,
    To show false Art what beauty was of yore.

Shakespeare, Sonnet 68

Contents

Acknowledgments

Every scholarly book is a complex collaboration, but a scholarly book on Jack Kerouac may be even more complex than most. Kerouac's status as a cult hero for three generations of Americans has created a network of aficionados, devotees, and collectors that constitutes an oral resource infinitely greater in volume and detail than the relatively refined collection of documents in even the most elaborate research library. One of the many distinct pleasures of writing this book lay in discovering the extent of the Kerouac network and in meeting many of the people who are active in it. Without the finely focused insights of the readers who keep Kerouac's writing alive outside the classroom, my work would have been difficult and, at best, unrewarding.

I want to thank particularly the faculty, staff, and students of the Naropa Institute in Boulder, Colorado, where I spent two exciting and productive summers. Anne Waldman, director of the Poetics Department at Naropa, actually made the suggestion that I come to Boulder in 1988 to work with Allen Ginsberg on what at that time promised to be merely a single essay on Kerouac's poetry. During the many hours we spent together that summer and the next, Allen gave me a rich practical insight into his most immediate poetic influence: the verse of Jack Kerouac. Many of Kerouac's old friends and associates who were passing through Boulder also took time to give me guidance. I owe special thanks in this respect to Gregory Corso, William S. Burroughs, Michael McClure, and Harry Smith, bishop of Boulder. Andy Hoffman and Eliot Greenspan handled many of the institutional arrangements for my two visits. Several young poets I met in Boulder who have been profoundly influenced by Kerouac helped me see the potential value of my work for future writers: Steve Creson, Tom Peters, Clint Frakes, Daniel Pirofsky, and Chris Ide (tell Jack in heaven that I've drunk my port wine, Chris). The library staff at Naropa also facilitated my access to the Institute's invaluable collection of tapes and ephemera relating to Kerouac, the Beats, and experimental writing in general.

Several other libraries and librarians also helped me ferret out the details of Kerouac's life and work that appear in the following pages. I am especially grateful to the staff of the Norlin Library at the University of Colorado for their assistance. The same goes for the special collections and reference librarians at the Bancroft Library at the University of California, Berkeley and the reference and English librarians at the University of Illinois.

Two summer faculty fellowships granted by the Office of Graduate Studies and Sponsored Research at Southwest Missouri State University provided the time that I needed to gather and assemble the material for this book. I also owe a debt to my friends, students, and colleagues in the English Department of Southwest Missouri State University. Among those who were kind enough to read and comment on preliminary drafts of this book were Bertha Harris, Jack Field, David Gann, and Tom Weis. I also thank Professor Mark Trevor Smith, who loaned me his copy of *A Buddhist Bible* for several years. Special thanks go to Professor Bill Burling and the graduate students in his research methods class during the fall semester of 1990 for helping me investigate some of the more esoteric references in several choruses of *Mexico City Blues*. I also appreciate the continued help, support, and advice of Professors Katherine Lederer and Robert H. Henigan, my two brilliant senior colleagues. My deepest gratitude, however, goes to Professor Linda Park-Fuller of the Southwest Missouri State University Department of Theater and Dance, whose 1985 production, *The Beats Go On*, inspired me to extend my fan's interest in Jack Kerouac's writing into the realm of scholarship. Without the impetus of Park-Fuller's script, this book—and the shift of scholarly attention that produced it—would have never come about.

1

Introduction

All that is, symbolizes.

"Between extremities / Man runs his course," Yeats wrote in "Vacillation" in an attempt to characterize the dialectic of his life and his art. Unlike the great Irish poet, the American writer Jack Kerouac never spoke so abstractly of the nature of his own personal or artistic conflicts. Nevertheless, like Yeats—like any true artist—Kerouac forged his art from paradox: he transformed the unalterable conditions of his existence into opposing sets of availing symbols, much like Blake's contraries. In doing so he provided himself with some necessary landmarks by which he guided the activity of his writing and perhaps the activity of self-exploration. At the same time, by erecting these guideposts in language, Kerouac made it possible for his readers to observe and appreciate his psychic struggle. The artful conflation of his personal

Each chapter begins with a quotation from Oswald Spengler's *Decline of the West* in order to suggest the influence of this germinal Modernist text on Kerouac's writing.

1

language with the traditional dialectic of literary symbolism, a sure
sign of his genius, makes it easier for us to evaluate objectively his
success as a writer. The primary purpose of this book is to provide
a guide to the most important ideas in *Mexico City Blues*, a ne-
glected major work by Kerouac, and to discuss these ideas in a
way that emphasizes their dialectical nature and affords a way into
the poem. While *Mexico City Blues* may seem immediately accessi-
ble as play on the simplest level, it probably will not be appreci-
ated even in this sense by most first-time readers. It may even be
perceived as a new *Waste Land*, full of hermetic knowledge pre-
sented in a convoluted style.

Aside from the complexity of the poem and the fact that it
has been largely ignored by Kerouac critics, I chose to focus my
discussion on *Mexico City Blues*, published by Grove Press in
1959, for two other reasons. First, the book makes a major contri-
bution to post-World War II poetry and poetics. But canons,
flexible and diverse as they may seem at present, remain hard to
revise in many respects, and Kerouac's reputation as a novelist
may prevent him from being considered an important poet. Un-
fortunate as this may be for the readers of future anthologies,
however, it does not alter the fact. Anyone who gives *Mexico City
Blues* an unbiased reading in the light of contemporary long
poems—*Paterson*, *Howl*, *The Dream Songs*, or *The Maximus Poems*,
for instance—will reach the same conclusion. Among the myster-
ies of literary prejudice remains the theorem that an author cannot
make major contributions to more than one genre, with its corol-
lary that a novelist cannot be a good poet. Nevertheless, *Mexico
City Blues* is a good poem, perhaps even a great one.

Another reason for discussing Kerouac's poetry is that it
sheds an interesting light on him as a writer. No American author
has received such intense interest from biographers in such a short
period of time. In the twenty-plus years since Jack Kerouac's
death in 1969, six book-length studies have appeared. These
books focus primarily on validating Kerouac's fiction by demon-
strating its basis in autobiography; despite this bias, none of them
has discovered any pattern in Kerouac's life that would provide a
rationale for evaluating his works in terms of their autobiographi-

cal significance. The biographers are stuck on a rather crude criterion of verisimilitude, which causes them to miss the forest on account of the trees.

The pattern I see in Kerouac's life is one familiar to many Americans and typical of American writers, especially in the twentieth century. Kerouac rose from an ethnic lower-middle-class background to notoriety as the "King of the Beatniks." He wanted simply to rise to a kind of romantic status as gentleman writer, but when he found different conditions of fame set by the media, he rejected them and reverted to his original status. Almost every conflict—including the sexual dynamic—of Kerouac's life can be understood as a result of his class attitudes. At a time when most writers wished to escape from class consciousness, Kerouac faithfully reported the intense and often painful struggle that led him from Lowell to New York and back.

Kerouac's fictional *annus mirabilis* was 1939 to 1940: he treats it in three different novels in the Duluoz Legend, *The Town and the City*, *Maggie Cassidy*, and *Vanity of Duluoz*. That was the year he left Lowell, discovered the city, and determined to become a writer. Given that 1939 was a watershed, it is possible to look at Kerouac's adult life in terms of his driving ambition to make his living by writing. As a direct result of this serious ambition, a conflict developed. Kerouac's view of his own art was uncompromising. Throughout the 1940s he worked unstintingly in a self-imposed apprenticeship. He was fond of boasting that by age twenty-one he had already written a million words. By the end of the decade he had composed four novels and a collection of short stories. In 1950 came his first publication, the Wolfean narrative of his separation from home and family and his first encounter with artists and bohemians in the city, *The Town and the City*. Kerouac's career was launched in the most typical way imaginable.

But it was all downhill from there, at least in terms of his romantic dreams of the writer's life. Because of his refusal to compromise his own innovative standards, he found himself at odds with the publishing establishment. He continued to write—sometimes furiously—but his next major publication, *On the Road*, was delayed for seven years. In the meantime, other conflicts in his life, many stemming from childhood, began to catch up with him. He drifted in and out of two brief marriages, then denied the daughter he had fathered by his second wife. Memories of his brother, Gerard, who died when Jack was only four, guilt over the death of his father, and feelings of responsibility for his aging mother began to overwhelm him. He became an alcoholic. During the mid-1950s, the darkest period of Kerouac's adult life, his commitment to art stood as the only stable feature of his life. It was at this time that he began to write poetry seriously, and in an important sense, *Mexico City Blues* is the culmination of an internalized crisis in Kerouac's life. However great the poem's merits as a work of literature, it must also be seen as definitive documentation of Kerouac's attempt to achieve both psychic and literary equilibrium. He endeavored to express in a complex, ritualized song as many symbols of his personal conflicts as he could effectively control by uniting them with traditional literary techniques. In this sense, *Mexico City Blues* is the most important book Kerouac ever wrote, and it sheds light on all his novels by providing a compendium of the issues that most concerned him as a writer, as well as a model for the transformation of conflict into an antiphonal language. Fans of Kerouac's fiction, who will have readier access to his poetic style, are likely to find in *Mexico City Blues* what Spengler called a counterworld, a sort of reversed image of Kerouac's narrative that throws a whole new light on his legend.

In what follows, I discuss Kerouac as poet in general, his use of autobiography in his writing, his attraction to Mexico, the importance of the blues in his writing, the influence of Buddhism on his life and work, his theory of spontaneous composition, and the form of *Mexico City Blues*, all in terms of the concert of opposites. Each chapter opens with a scene from one of Kerouac's novels to underscore the relevance and connection of the topic at hand to all of Kerouac's work. Finally, chapters 3 through 8 are each divided into two parts: the first is a discussion of major themes in *Mexico City Blues*; the second, a detailed reading of the poem from the perspective of the chapter's topic.

I chose the metaphor of the map to govern my discussion here for several reasons. First, I wanted to suggest a spatial dimension for the narrative and lyric qualities of *Mexico City Blues*. This poem takes on many of the qualities of the place in which it was written. By place I mean both Mexico City and Kerouac's imagination. Second, I wanted the metaphor to characterize my own role as a critic. Rather than casting myself as a tour guide, I prefer to see myself as a cartographer. *Mexico City Blues*, even for most Kerouac fans, is *terra incognita*, and even for one who has been there many times, I must say that it is a strange land. It never becomes completely familiar, and that is one of its undeniable charms. Something new always lies in store for even the most experienced traveler. The point is to make sure readers know they can find their way around the poem without the actual physical presence of a tour guide. Maps, as we know, are far from being completely objective instruments, but they are unquestionably useful, despite their cultural biases and occasional factual errors.

Third, I wanted to suggest to Kerouac readers a way of orienting themselves in this and in other Kerouac texts. The topics I chose to discuss are, for me, like directions. (That there are more than four merely suggests finer gradations on the compass, or perhaps a surreal geography, in which the traveler, as in *Gulliver's Travels*, is permitted to leave the flat plane of the earth for a while.) Each topic has its antipodes, with a more or less highly detailed territory stretched between. The poles, which were once exclusively Kerouac's, now belong to all of us. His imaginings described the farthest reaches of his spirit, and I wish merely to use them as compass points to enable readers to orient themselves in the poem. What discoveries are to be made depend on the character of the individual traveler. In any case, the opposed points of the compass that govern the map are meant to provide stability, to keep us from getting lost. As Jung said in his essay "On the Nature of the Psyche": "The ego keeps its integrity only if it does not identify with one of the opposites, and if it understands how to hold a balance between them. This is possible only if it remains conscious of both at once" (89). In *Mexico City Blues* the reader may observe Kerouac keeping his most precarious balance, and although he quickly lost his equilibrium after the publication of *On the Road*, in this long poem he managed to articulate and array the most serious conflicts of his life as pairs of opposites and to maintain his stability as an artist and as a human being by remaining conscious of both extremes at once. In this difficult and exciting act of balance, Kerouac, like Yeats, provides us with a model of art and, perhaps, of life.

2

The Novelist as Poet

*All a man's sensations or misunderstandings, faith or knowledge, receive
their shape from a primary opposition which makes them not only activities
of the individual, but also expressions of the totality.*

Among a series of bohemian literary debates in his novel *The
Subterraneans* (written in 1953), Kerouac recounts an argu-
ment with the poet Gregory Corso, who is disguised as the
story's antagonist, Yuri Gligoric. Kerouac himself plays the charac-
ter of Leo Percepied, a name which combines his father's given
name with the French equivalent of Oedipus:

> Yuri and I'd had a long talk that week in a bar, over port
> wines, he claimed everything was poetry, I tried to make the
> common old distinction between verse and prose, he said, "Lis-
> sen Percepied do you believe in freedom? then say what you
> want, it's poetry, poetry, all of it is poetry, great prose is po-
> etry, great verse is poetry."—"Yes" I said "but verse is verse and
> prose is prose."—"No no" he yelled "it's all poetry."—"Okay," I
> said, "I believe in you believing in freedom and maybe you're
> right, have another wine." (114)

It seems strange to hear the Kerouac character maintaining the traditional distinction, especially since his articulation of it, which sounds at once both weak and dogmatic, precedes by only a few sentences his insistence that "Yuri" employ the spontaneous method in the composition of his own poetry. Though there is more than meets the eye to Leo's assertion that "verse is verse and prose is prose," on some level Kerouac is probably honestly expressing his belief in all its simplicity. Finally, this bare assertion of fact is all the evidence he gives to account for the most profound and perplexing distinction in the history of literature.

It is not unusual for novelists to write poetry, although among the Modernists it seems to be a kind of juvenile or at least preliminary literary activity. Not many prose writers begin, as Kerouac did, to devote serious attention to poetry only in midcareer. Of course, Kerouac had been writing poetry all along, even since childhood. His first poem was composed for a classmate in parochial school, and his first literary pal in high school, Sammy Sampas (who is alluded to in the "47th Chorus" of *Mexico City Blues*), was a great fan of Byron and the other Romantic poets. Kerouac's first publication came, ironically, under the editorship of his primary poetic influence, his lifelong friend Allen Ginsberg. In 1945, Ginsberg, as editor of the Columbia University *Jester*, translated a French text of Kerouac and published it under the pseudonym "Jean Louis Incogniteau." Typical of Kerouac's career, even this seemingly inauspicious beginning has great symbolic significance. It was not to poetry, however, that Kerouac devoted the great outburst of creative energy characterizing the period from 1944 to 1954, but to fiction—a fiction that moved rapidly and surely away from its Romantic origins in the imitation of Thomas Wolfe through a series of other carefully considered literary, historical, and psychological models.

Even in its origins, however, Kerouac's fiction is far from pure. As much as he admired Wolfe, he also fancied Hemingway. He liked the short works of Saroyan, but he quickly discovered— and decided to emulate—the sagas of Galsworthy. Kerouac learned from Wolfe not so much a style—he abandoned his imitation in the course of a single novel—but a bias, a bias toward the

8

sound of words. Because Kerouac tended to de-emphasize content, his career as a novelist may on a superficial level look like a restless attempt to resolve fundamental conflicts by changing their names from story to story. His first published novel, *The Town and the City*, takes its title from Spengler's notion in *The Decline of the West* (in a chapter titled "The Soul of the City") that one characteristic of the shift from culture to civilization—and therefore of the culture's approaching demise—is the supersession of the city over the town (2:87). Kerouac saw the downfall of culture recapitulated in his own life when his family was forced to move from Lowell to New York City. Ironically, this move was, for Kerouac as a writer, a necessary and vital liberation. But it was his own ambivalence that stuck in his mind.

In many ways, *On the Road*, whose stylistic model was the then unpublished writing—if not the actual doings—of Neal Cassady, presents the counterargument to Spengler's vision of decline (McNally 133); at the same time, *On the Road* finds the dark side of Cassady's exuberance in his ruthless selfishness. It exchanges cultural polarities for personal ones, and the East-West pendular swings of the journeys in the novel are simply emblems of ambivalence. Even this early in his career, Mexico represented for Kerouac a resolution of opposites: return to the peasant culture—Spengler's fellaheen—and solitude in the city. In his other version of Cassady's adventures, *Visions of Cody*, Kerouac managed to transmute his conflict into artistic terms. Gerald Nicosia describes the "pivoting of the book between subjective illusions of sight and sound" and praises this as a highly effective means of organization (387). Kerouac's breakthrough into spontaneous composition in 1951 had apparently given him the aesthetic means to balance the oppositions he felt so strongly in his life.

Kerouac certainly did not swerve from his confrontation with the duality. *Dr. Sax*, in fact, takes up the gauntlet in classic Spenglerian terms by attempting to extend the drama of Faust into a third part. According to Spengler (1:354), the two parts of Goethe's *Faust* represent characterizations of two centuries, the eighteenth and nineteenth, solitary introspection versus practical activity, and Kerouac was undoubtedly contributing his characterization of our own century as either a balance between the two poles or an escape from polarity altogether. He even imports Aztec mythology to mediate the traditional Christian dualism.

It is fascinating that Kerouac began *Maggie Cassidy*, an attempt to reconcile his personal sexual needs with his public social needs in terms of Catholicism, before he discovered that the Aztec mythology would not avail him here. In *The Subterraneans*, under the influence of Dostoevsky's instinctive psychological orientation, Kerouac tried to understand the madness of life by playing off Reich's theory of orgasm (which, like Spengler's theory of the decline of the West, was taught to him by William S. Burroughs) against Freudian analysis. This novel, which epitomizes the spontaneous style, sets the stage for Kerouac's discovery of Buddhism in early 1954, the only year between 1951 and 1957 in which he did not write at least one novel.

Kerouac's self-conversion to Buddhism is the most important single event in his life in terms of its effect on his art. His inclination toward its monastic view of life is clear as early as *The Town and the City* in the character of Frances Martin (modeled after Ivan in *The Brothers Karamazov*); similarly, *Tristessa*, written in two parts during the summers of 1955 and 1956, constitutes a revision of *Maggie Cassidy* from the perspective of Buddhist asceticism. *Desolation Angels*, also written in two parts—although this time the parts were separated not by one year but by five—employs a balance of Catholicism and Buddhism to stabilize the oscillation between solitude and society Duluoz experiences. Here again, the protagonist's little rooftop dwelling in Mexico City seems to represent the perfect balance, unlike the horror of nine weeks in a fire lookout on top of a mountain.

This is the period—1954 to 1957—that spawned *Mexico City Blues*, the most thoroughly and undeservedly ignored of Kerouac's major works. The poem itself is a complex product of the development of Kerouac's fictional technique—spontaneous prose—and of his excitement over the newfound vocabulary of Buddhism. It also results in part from Kerouac's curious resignation about his failure to publish any of his novels after *The Town and the City*. His engagement with Buddhism, spurred by the resistance of Neal and Carolyn Cassady's obsession with the teachings of Edgar Cayce, had the inexplicable side effect of causing him to take a much more serious interest in writing poetry. The first full book Kerouac wrote after beginning his reading of Asvaghosa's *Acts of the Buddha* and Dwight Goddard's *Buddhist Bible* was a sequence of poems called *San Francisco Blues* (written in 1954). About this time he conceived a poetic equivalent to his fictional saga, the Duluoz Legend. He intended to join all his poems in a "Book of Blues." The first installment, *San Francisco Blues*, shows Kerouac tuning his powers of observation; however, without the strong narrative thrust of his fiction, the individual poems—though often successful individually—flounder in an arbitrary progression. But a little over a year later, in *Mexico City Blues*, Kerouac managed to apply his fifteen-year-old appreciation of jazz to create a form that would sustain for over two hundred pages not only acute introspection, but serious theological speculation as well.

Besides writing poetry and fiction, Kerouac filled the mid-1950s by composing religious texts. Only one of these, *The Scripture of the Golden Eternity*, his own American sutra, has yet been published. This work has special aesthetic signficance because he exempted it from the restrictions of his spontaneous method of composition, believing that because it was a scripture, he had no right to impose his style on it. He also wrote his own biography of Buddha and compiled his notes and musings on Buddhism into a text called *Some of the Dharma*. Then, in January 1956, Kerouac returned to writing fiction. In ten nights in the kitchen of his sister's home in North Carolina, under the influence of alcohol, benzedrine, and Shakespeare's history plays, he wrote *Visions of Gerard*, his attempt to understand the first major tragedy of his life in terms of the Buddhist doctrine of suffering. It is no accident that *Visions of Gerard* is also Kerouac's most profoundly Catholic novel, since one effect of his study of Buddhism was to bring the influence of his childhood religion into a perfect equipoise. His specifically Buddhist period concludes with *The Dharma Bums*, written in 1957 after the publication of *On the Road*. This novel, which some critics consider a potboiler written to cash in on the notoriety of *On the Road*, is more accurately described as a revision of the previous novel to include the insights Kerouac gained through his study of Buddhism. He gained these insights in part by substituting Gary Snyder—a woodsman, a student of Zen, and most importantly, a poet—for Neal Cassady, the "cocksman and Adonis of Denver" (*Howl* 14), to use Ginsberg's words, as hero.

The advent of Kerouac's fame around the end of 1957 destroyed the three-year period of grace he enjoyed largely as a result of his Buddhist studies. The more his notoriety increased, the more his life became a struggle to maintain his own stability. He continued to write poetry, some of which he published in small magazines and Catholic periodicals, but his verse never regained the sustained power and continuity of *Mexico City Blues*, and he concentrated more on haiku in his declining years. As a testimony to Kerouac's tenacity and as an epitaph to his loss of balance, he managed to write *Big Sur*, the story of his alcoholic breakdown, in 1961. *Big Sur* weighs heavy with the pathos of loss, but it also marks a belated attempt to fuse fiction and verse in the twenty-page poem that concludes the book. After this Kerouac managed to write only two other novels: *Satori in Paris*, which nominally attempts to reinject a saving Buddhism into his life and fiction, and *Vanity of Duluoz*, which fills in the fictional legend of his life by focusing on his days as an athlete in high school and college, the days of his early triumph, abandoned for the sake of literature.

Mexico City Blues is the fulfillment of Kerouac's spontaneous poetics, a poetics that, because of the nature of realistic narrative, could not be completely fulfilled in fiction. Just as Buddhism neutralized many of the psychological constraints of Catholicism, so the medium of poetry liberated Kerouac's artistic intuition from the severest restrictions of narrative sequence. That is, *Mexico City Blues* creates much the same effect as *Visions of Cody*, but the conventions of the poetic medium—concision, ellipsis, imagery, sound effects—make the product much more elegant. Kerouac may be the only example in literature of a novelist whose fictional technique led him directly to poetry. If I make extravagant claims for the importance of *Mexico City Blues*, it is partly because the poem bears out those claims, and partly because I see Kerouac's poetry and fiction as all of a piece. Leo's argument with Yuri in *The Subterraneans* sounds weak because he does not really believe it. He is arguing with Yuri because Yuri is his rival, in both love and poetry. Leo thinks that he himself is a better lover and a better poet, but secretly he believes with Yuri that prose and verse are one.

All of the Kerouac biographies—McNally's most insistently—substantiate the notion that Kerouac's mind was deeply divided in terms of gender, race, ethnicity, class, and religion. From the time of his obsession with "self-ultimacy" and with Lucien Carr's "New Vision" based on the system of Yeats, in the mid-1940s, to his search for a "deep form" that combined vertical and horizontal movement, through his discovery of the spontaneous method and the technique of "sketching" in 1951, it also appears that Kerouac's poetics reflected the other conflicts of his mind. His manifestos contain images of opposition between circumference and center, memory and scene, narration and description, unconscious and conscious, internal and external. In critical retrospect, he seems to have been working to set up a system of polarities that would balance against one another while he moved between them with his speculations, as Krishna and Arjuna moved between the two armies on the battlefield in the *Bhagavad Gita*.

But the twofold demand of his art—to reach back in his memory to discover his own origin and to reach out into the world around him to discover its meaning—threatened to tear him apart. Only motion was capable of sustaining the balance. Like a tightrope walker, Kerouac was always edging forward or gingerly backing up. To remain still would have caused a life-threatening fall. In his poetics the equivalent of motion is talk. Kerouac's orality, learned growing up in a relatively antiliterate culture, encouraged him to generate sound continually. Fortunately, when he left home, he found other subcultures equally fond of talk. Whether they were bohemian or working-class, the bars he loved to frequent surrounded him with the perpetual motion of speech.

From Thomas Wolfe he learned not only to conceptualize and romanticize his existence, but also, more importantly, to listen to the sound of the words he wrote. He told his high school pals that he was going to become a writer, and he "practiced with his mouth" (McNally 23). Nicosia explains that Kerouac "would repeat a piece of written or spoken language until people finally *listened* to it." Then, "if someone protested that he had already heard it, Kerouac would tell him to 'hear more'" (184). His intense interest in music, likewise, taught him ways to manipulate sound beyond regard for meaning. "Listening to Bird [bop saxophonist Charlie Parker]—and he did so constantly—," McNally says, "Kerouac felt myriad connections of subject, style, and approach, and tried to reflect that aural perfection in his own prose" (148). By the mid-1950s, as Gary Snyder has testified, Kerouac had made the transference, and the reciprocal effect was that "conversation with Kerouac was always, strictly speaking, poetical" (Gifford and Lee 212). Later, when alcohol began to exact its toll on Kerouac's writing, his creative fusion of speech and writing fell apart, and he sought refuge in saloons: "Because of the massive emotional paralysis of his writer's block, Kerouac had turned from the solitary act of writing to the direct communication of talk. The two modes contradicted each other" (McNally 320).

At the pinnacle of his career—that is, just before he achieved the fame that followed the publication of *On the Road*, Kerouac's writing *became* speech. From the tape transcriptions of *Visions of Cody* to "tape, the new kind of voice" in the "172nd Chorus" of *Mexico City Blues*, Kerouac developed his native orality into a sophisticated poetics. His great urge to speak led him through the contradictions that often frustrated his full response in other arenas of life, and while his emphasis on sound did not eliminate the polarities of his existence, it did resolve them momentarily in an expression of the senses. The oppositions that create tension are obvious in his fiction and his poetry. His voice gives this tension direction and runs like a unifying current through his works. In learning how to write, Kerouac really learned to sing, to transform his speech into art. His song is both the balance between the contradictions of his life and the unity in the diversity of his works, a fusion of poetry and prose.

In proportion to all the poetry Kerouac wrote, very little has been published. At present, we have no way of ascertaining the full dimensions of his "Book of Blues," the projected equivalent of his fictional Duluoz Legend, but from what has reached print we can gather an outline of his achievement as a poet.

If it had not been for Kenneth Rexroth's vicious review of *Mexico City Blues* in the *New York Times*, the only book of Kerouac's poetry published during his lifetime might have gone completely unnoticed in the popular press. Rexroth, who was hardly known for pulling punches, unleashed the full measure of his irrational fury on Kerouac's poem without appreciating in the least what Kerouac was trying to accomplish. Whether Rexroth was really castigating Kerouac for his bad manners at Rexroth's San Francisco salon or trying to get at Kerouac's friend, the poet Robert Creeley, who had had an affair with Rexroth's wife, or merely venting some private frustration in literary terms, the *Times* piece is a model of unethical behavior in print. For Creeley's part, he defended Kerouac's work in a shotgun review in *Poetry*, but the terms of his defense are ambiguous. The best immediate response to *Mexico City Blues* came from an unexpected quarter, a review by the poet and satirist Anthony Hecht in the mainstream literary journal *The Hudson Review*. Hecht not only gives the good advice that the poem should be read in one sitting—implying that it is a unified presentation—but he also perceives its literariness, pointing out Kerouac's debt to Pound, Stein, Williams, cummings, Joyce, and even Eliot. Despite Hecht's perceptive praise, however, Rexroth's diatribe in the middle-brow media consigned one of Kerouac's richest works to temporary obscurity.

During the last decade of his life, Kerouac continued to write and publish in the small magazines, thus lending his name to many avant-garde and underground publications. As he grew more outspoken in his conservatism and Catholicism, he also began to send poems to the Catholic magazine *Jubilee*. The first collection of his magazine publications was compiled by Kerouac's first biographer, Ann Charters, and published by City Lights in 1971 under the title *Scattered Poems*. Along with the previously published work, Charters also included several poems extracted from Kerouac's letters to Allen Ginsberg. Apparently, it had long been his practice to include poems in his letters to friends (Gifford and Lee 236). *Scattered Poems* is valuable primarily because its contents cover the entire quarter century of Kerouac's literary career, from 1945 to 1969. One chorus of *Mexico City Blues* even sneaks in untitled and with several alterations in the text. This is the "236th Chorus," which begins: "The Buddhist Saints are the incomparable saints" (*Scattered Poems* 25).

Compared with the variety of *Scattered Poems*, especially the concluding section of haikus, Don Allen's 1977 collection for Grey Fox Press, *Heaven & Other Poems*, gives a strong sense of the two basic tendencies of Kerouac's verse. As Allen's editorial correspondence in this volume makes clear, Kerouac recognized his own propensity for the poetic sequence. He spent a good deal of time trying to arrange his sequences and to make sure they were kept in tact when published. *Heaven*, in fact, reprints the eight choruses from *Mexico City Blues* that were published in Allen's landmark 1960 anthology, *New American Poetry*. Here, Kerouac tried to give them another kind of organization by replacing the chorus numbers with colors. The "202nd Chorus," for instance, becomes "White Pome." The others are colored Rose, Black, Gray, Blue, Green, Red, and Brown, giving the excerpted choruses a new order with reference to Kerouac's color symbolism, perhaps indicating a regression to childhood. (The other chorus numbers in the order in which they occur in *Heaven* are: 104, 119, 120, 135, 141, 160, and 176, an indication that Kerouac also wished to preserve their order in the original sequence.)

Heaven & Other Poems also contains sections from some of Kerouac's other sequences, for which he gave the dates of composition in a letter to Don Allen (50). "McDougal Street Blues," written in 1955 just before Kerouac left for Mexico City, bears the strongest resemblance to *Mexico City Blues*. Nicosia says that Kerouac had just read Pound's *Cantos* in Greenwich Village, "but his initial enthusiasm for the freedom of the poetry [evidenced by the organization of "MacDougal Street Blues"] soon dissolved in his disgust for Pound's pretentious diction and imitation of classical rhythms" (475). Kerouac's resistance to Pound's Modernism must have been so sharp and immediate that it caused him to solidify, in the space of a mere few weeks, the notion of the improvisational structure of repeating choruses.

He had, it appears from another letter in *Heaven* (56), intended to employ that structure from the very beginning in *San*

Francisco Blues, but it is unclear to me whether or not he grasped its significance until after his great success with it in *Mexico City Blues*. In any case, his composition of other sequences such as "Orizaba Blues," named after the street he lived on in Mexico City, and "Orlando Blues," commemorating his home in Florida, suggests that, regardless of the exact structure he used, his intuition led him toward a melding of the short, lyric unit into a long sequence with narrative potential. Although he did attempt long poems without any kind of standard unit of internal division—as evidenced by the biographical narrative "Rimbaud" (*Scattered Poems* 32); the eight-page poem, "Heaven" (*Heaven* 23); and the lengthy non-narrative poem, "Sea," at the conclusion of *Big Sur* (219–41)—both his inclination and his forte seemed to lie in a more complex form.

"Sea," however, provides a late example of Kerouac's poetic stamina. Taking his cue from James Joyce, Kerouac set out to record the sounds of the Pacific Ocean near Big Sur in Northern California. He had also intended, it appears, to write a similar poem about the Atlantic when he traveled to his ancestral home in Brittany. "Sea" displays many of the same themes as *Mexico City Blues*, and the prevalence of French in the poem foretells the pathos of Kerouac's late obsession with his ethnic heritage, an obsession chronicled in painful detail in *Satori in Paris*. It also brings into high relief another aspect of Kerouac's emphasis on the sound of words: his attempt to limn the noises in nature. "Sea" is punctuated by subtle variations the singer hears in the crashing waves and reproduces in human music. Kerouac's concern with the conflicts of his own life surfaces here, as usual. "I'll have a daughter, / oughter, wait & seee," the singer muses (*Big Sur* 230). The roar of the surf works like a mirror of sound that elicits all the most resonant memories and powerful feelings. The singer recognizes the futility of his own (pre)occupation: "No human words bespeak / the token sorrow older / than old this wave" (223). Predictably, the poem takes on a religious significance. Rather than the form of a quest, as in *Mexico City Blues*, however, "Sea" proposes a simple inquiry. The ocean is the singer's correspondent, collaborator, and enemy as well. Near the end, the singer musters his Buddhist resources to make an assertion of success, which stands in stark contrast to the alcoholic disaster retold in the novel: "My golden empty soul'll / outlast yr salty sill" (239). This is proof, I think, that despite his preference for the poetic sequence, Kerouac could sustain, with some confidence, a lengthy non-narrative poem.

The West Coast poet Gary Snyder once recalled a comment made by Allen Ginsberg that "Kerouac was about the only one we knew who was able to spontaneously compose *haiku* that wasn't boring, without sitting on it for a long time" (Gifford and Lee 211). Kerouac's talent for haiku represents the complementary impulse to his desire to create extended sequences. These poles are analogous to those of his fictional "deep form," with its twin goals of vertical description and horizontal narrative. Kerouac discovered haiku during his initial Buddhist studies, and the form continued to have a religious connotation for the rest of his career. Nicosia finds that many of the prose lines of *Visions of Gerard* are really haiku (501), and Kerouac interpolates haiku into the prose of *The Dharma Bums*. He maintained his interest at least through 1967, when he composed haiku spontaneously for Ted Berrigan as he conducted an interview for *The Paris Review*. Besides the concluding section in *Scattered Poems* and a single haiku in *Heaven & Other Poems*, a few of Kerouac's haikus can be found in *Trip Trap*, a collaboration done in 1959 with Lew Welch and Albert Saijo, and in *American Haikus*, a fine press transcript of the haiku performed by Kerouac on his LP *Blues and Haikus*, published by Caliban Press (no date).

Interest in publishing Kerouac's poetry has continued long after his death. The complete sequence of *San Francisco Blues*, Kerouac's first book of poetry and the first thing he wrote after discovering Buddhism, was published in a limited edition by Beat Books in 1983. The "language-spinning" (*Big Sur* 124), the playfulness, and the musicality are all evident in this early work, though Buddhism has only begun to show signs of emerging; however, the most distinctive quality of the poem is its naturalistic imagery, carried over from Kerouac's fictional technique of sketching, but transformed by the rapid shifts of his surrealist poetics. The poem contains some high moments, such as chorus "(25)" or these lines from chorus "(75)":

Secret
Poetry
Deceives
Simply.

What is lacking is not to be found in the individual choruses, which sustain interest independently, but rather in the book as a whole. The themes, images, and sounds do not coalesce, and the poem, quite simply, is not long enough to make full use of the improvisational technique. It is a step toward *Mexico City Blues*, but unlike "MacDougal Street Blues"—which closely anticipates the finesse of the poems Kerouac wrote later that same summer of 1955—*San Francisco Blues* is a preliminary step.

One other source of information about Kerouac's poems must be cited: his sound recordings. The extant ones were all made in 1959, and together they contain a number of choruses from *Mexico City Blues* and the other sequences Kerouac presumably intended to gather eventually into his "Book of Blues." Here, over the piano playing of author, comedian, and television personality Steve Allen, or with the counterpoint of saxophone riffs by Zoot Sims and Al Cohn, the listener gets an opportunity to gauge the grain of Kerouac's voice. One is reminded of his origins by his strong New England accent. One gets a sense of his rhythm and intonation and a feel for his tempo. Best of all, however, one gets to hear the articulation of the consonants and vowels—above all the open *o*'s and *u*'s that carry much of the melody in *Mexico City Blues*. The contents of the original records, some outtakes, and a recording of Kerouac's public appearance at Brandeis University were released as a boxed set by Rhino Records in 1990. Anyone who doubts the unifying capacity of Kerouac's voice should give these recordings serious attention.

When City Lights publisher Lawrence Ferlinghetti rejected the "Book of Blues" (the manuscript of which is still apparently in his possession) on the grounds that it didn't qualify as poetry, Kerouac was outraged, according to Nicosia: "Although Kerouac himself was aware of the prosaic tendencies of his poetry—and felt that he could say what he wanted more exactly in prose—he was always outraged to hear similar criticism coming from someone

else" (564). Once, in a letter to James Laughlin, founder of New
Directions, Kerouac explained: "All my books are as it were po-
etry sheeted in narrative steel" (Nicosia 545). Kerouac reportedly
admired Poe's prose style, "perhaps because Poe observed slight
distinction between poetry and prose, as did Kerouac himself"
(Nicosia 307). In Kerouac's work, as in his own thinking, the dis-
tinction between prose and poetry becomes problematic. He de-
nies it as he maintains it, and his reader is left wondering whether
the distinction has anything other than typographical significance.
Ferlinghetti's remark on this matter is worth quoting in full.

> I think he was a better novel writer than a poem writer. I'm
> putting it that way because it seems to me that the writing he
> did was all one, whether it was in the topography of poetry or
> in the topography of prose. It was the same kind of writing. If
> it were read aloud it sounded the same. It was poetry and vice
> versa. Right there the distinction between poetry and prose
> broke down. (Gifford and Lee 271)

While I disagree with Ferlinghetti's value judgment, I concur
completely with his reasoning, which seems to contradict his con-
clusion. I think the reader who is familiar with Kerouac's prose
will find in his poetry the same preoccupations—autobiography,
travel, music, religion, spontaneity—woven into an even denser
fabric. Each of these preoccupations involves its own conflicts, and
in his poems Kerouac managed to transform the conflicts into
"contraries"—as Blake would call them—and to bring them into
precarious balance. The rush of his prose, like running between
raindrops, is reified in the structure of the poetic sequence. The
sketching produces images instead of scenes, but the elemental op-
position he sought in deep form remains. "Verse is verse," as Leo
tells Yuri, "and prose is prose," but the twain do meet in Kerouac,
and this is one of the reasons his poetry is important. It is an ob-
ject lesson in Postmodern aesthetics.

On a purely literary level, Kerouac's poetry is worth reading
for two reasons. First, it extends and refines the tradition of the
sequence poem, which had its origins in love poetry and found its
finest form in the sonnet. Second, it provides a counterworld—to

repeat Spengler's term—to his prose. What is narrative drive in Kerouac's novels becomes fluid form in *Mexico City Blues*. I think this is a masterful transmutation. Further, he composed *Mexico City Blues*, as Allen Ginsberg explained to John Ryan in August 1955, "at the height of his romantic sense of himself" (qtd. in Charters 386). I think anyone who gives the poem a thorough reading will discover that it may also mark the height of Kerouac's power as a writer. For me, it represents the zenith of his career. It makes an important statement about the role of Mexico in Beat literature, provides a dramatic synthesis of Kerouac's Buddhist studies, draws the clearest formal analogy between jazz and literature, and presents a tutorial in the nuances of the complicated method of spontaneous composition. For admirers of Kerouac, it is a hidden gem. For admirers of Postmodern literature, it is an unheralded classic.

Gerald Nicosia expresses the opinion that "Kerouac's *Blues* is one of the most important poetic works in the second half of the twentieth century" (460). I think *Mexico City Blues* by itself is worthy of that accolade. Though Kerouac's reputation as a novelist has obscured the value of his poetry, the oral quality of his prose leads one surely back to his verse. The sound of human speech is what Kerouac strove to capture in his fiction, and the sound of human speech is what unifies his most accomplished poem. It is also the sound of human speech that resolves the many conflicting themes of his works and makes his prose and poetry, finally, one.

3

Auto/Biography

Truth in the long run is to him the picture of the world which was born at his birth. . . . It is that which he does not invent but rather discovers within himself. It is himself over and over again: his being expressed in words; the meaning of his personality formed into a doctrine which so far as concerns his life is unalterable, because truth and his life are identical.

The experienced reader of Kerouac's novels comes to expect the kind of scenes that fill *Vanity of Duluoz*, the last complete novel Kerouac wrote. In the most sincere and forthright tone, for instance, the first-person narrator recounts a significant incident of his early college days:

> I lighted a candle, cut a little into my finger, dripped blood, and wrote "The Blood of the Poet" on a little calling card, with ink, then the big word "BLOOD" over it, and hung that up on the wall as reminder of my new calling. "Blood" writ in blood. (202)

Such passionate confessions, so reminiscent of Rousseau, so replete with Romantic emotions, typify Kerouac's fiction. It is difficult for a friendly reader—who is apt to identify with all of Kerouac's narrators—to gain any distance from this description of the beginning of Kerouac's "Self Ultimacy" period, during which he burned at night whatever he had written during the day. This narrowing of distance between writer and reader is compounded by the blurring of the distinction between fact and fiction. Readers are frequently attracted to Kerouac's writing by its willingness to reveal the intimate details of the author's consciousness, and this initial attraction subsequently locks these readers into biographical interpretations of the texts. What is lost in this kind of interpretation, it seems to me, is an appreciation of Kerouac's mastery of technique and form, both fictional and poetic.

Despite the residual prejudices of the New Criticism and the current availability of a wide array of exciting critical theories, readers of Kerouac still tend to come at his writing by way of his life. Whatever the limitations of this biographical bias, it understandably derives from three related sources: the first is Kerouac's own insistence on truth in his writing; the other, more closely related sources are Allen Ginsberg and the media.

In the late 1940s, even as he worked to complete *The Town and the City*—his fourth novel, though the first to be published—Kerouac began to grow dissatisfied with the conventional techniques and aims of fiction; indeed, he began to reject the very premise of fiction. The stories he wanted to tell, it seemed to him, were all true. He recalled Spengler's pronouncement about Goethe, that great writers simply confess the stories of their own lives (1:13). Like Spengler, Kerouac understood that the only objectivity possible in art comes from perfect fidelity to subjectivity. And Kerouac had read Goethe's autobiography; he, too, identified poetry with truth. Consequently, Kerouac began to question the need for disguises in his fictions. Why, he asked himself, must an author invent names for characters who are obviously depictions of people in his own life? Why must he change settings, construct scenes, fabricate action? In effect, why couldn't a contemporary novelist, in the great tradition of Romantic confession, simply write his own autobiography?

These and other fundamental questions soon led Kerouac away from realism into an experimental mode geared toward the production of sound and rhythm in prose. He found his antecedents in James Joyce and Thomas Wolfe, but his own beginner's uncertainty about this experimentation caused him to protest too much that his stories, however innovative they might sound, were nevertheless pure reflections of reality as he lived it.

While Kerouac was apparently very naive about the legal advantages of changing the names to protect the innocent and the guilty, I doubt that he was nearly so naive about his ability to accomplish his own fictional aims. Despite his phenomenal memory, which he coupled with his skill as a speed-typist to capture the wealth of detail produced simultaneously by his recollections and his impressions, he was constantly aware of how much he was missing. And despite his grand—or perhaps even grandiose— schemes to write novels that "explained everything to everybody" and to construct a legend that would encompass the narrative of his whole life, Kerouac felt with excruciating sensitivity the pressure to limit and select. Ironically, given his later reputation for sexual explicitness, his selectivity is most notable when he deals with the sex lives of his friends, friends he has thinly disguised as characters. Possessed himself of an old-fashioned Catholic modesty, Kerouac was quite ready to omit a revealing or embarrassing detail from his "true" stories. And this is only the most obvious example of his fictional selectivity.

The point is that Kerouac's theory varied from his practice. This theory, articulated in two brief manifestos about spontaneous writing, served a psychological as much as an aesthetic purpose. His insistence on fidelity to facts in storytelling freed him to follow the cadence of the sounds in his settings, the speech mannerisms of his characters, the voice he was in the process of creating for himself. His claims of absolutely accurate mimesis—which are justified only in the strict Spenglerian sense of objective subjectivity—helped Kerouac convince himself that his innovation had a firm basis in substance, in truth. Unfortunately, his theory also functioned only too effectively as propaganda. During his brief period of fame in the late 1950s, this propaganda had severe negative consequences, both personally and critically. Conservative critics—and there were not many other kinds at the time—construed his depictions of his reality to be arguments in favor of the kind of behavior he described. Fans wanted to get in on the fun.

The envious wanted to chalk up a point by duking it out with the King of the Beats.

The propaganda effects of Kerouac's poetics crop up frequently in biographies and criticism. More often than not, commentators use passages in Kerouac's fiction to amplify details of his life, rather than the other way round. The cumulative effect is not so much wrong as it is simply distracting. It distracts from Kerouac's genuine contribution to Postmodern poetics: his emphasis on orality over literacy, on music rather than on representation, on the semiotic rather than on the symbolic, to use Kristeva's terms (92–93). This is not to say that biographical information plays no role in the interpretation of *Mexico City Blues* or any other Kerouac work for that matter, but that such information merely provides a means—like any other theme that makes the poem cohere—of orchestration and organization. In the second half of this chapter, I will try to read the autobiographical content of the poem without undermining Kerouac's poetics.

Briefly then, the other, more closely related sources of biographical bias in the reading of Kerouac's works are Allen Ginsberg and the media. Ginsberg's campaign for a united front of avant-garde American poets began in October 1955, almost immediately after his public debut at the famous Six Gallery reading, where he first performed the newly composed "Howl." His efforts to organize were resisted by most of the West Coast poets associated with the Beats, especially the leader of the previous generation of San Francisco writers, Kenneth Rexroth, and the heavily Olson-influenced Robert Duncan. Gary Snyder, Philip Whalen, and Michael McClure, however, though they strove to maintain separate identities, were less reluctant to join Ginsberg's movement.

Ginsberg was probably the first poet in America since Walt Whitman to create a full-blown media campaign on his own behalf. He was certainly the first to use the newly matured techniques of public relations. His several years of training in the media and in market research, combined with his relentless energy and talkativeness, virtually ensured the success of his campaign. Within two years of the Six Gallery reading, Ginsberg was well on his way to being an easily recognized public figure, the San Francisco Renaissance had become an accepted fact of literary history, and the circle of Ginsberg's close friends had been canonized by the media as the Beats.

For almost a decade, of course, Ginsberg strove to promote the work of his friends, Kerouac, Burroughs, and Cassady, among others. In fact, he served as unpaid agent for all three writers at one time or another, and he was directly responsible for the placement of Burroughs's first novel, *Junky*. Ginsberg also shared and helped develop Kerouac's poetics of absolute frankness and veracity. The aura of honesty and candor that emanated from the Beats as a group fortified the intensity of each member. If Kerouac's apology for honesty was limited to his personal contacts, Ginsberg's was not. Ginsberg's honesty, a figurative and often literal nakedness, was taken up by the media, which used it to characterize, sensationalize, and victimize the Beats.

When *On the Road*, Kerouac's second published novel, hit the best-seller list in late 1957, Ginsberg was out of the country, having already begun his own epic travels. Partly because of the circumstances of publication, partly because of his good looks, and partly by default, then, Kerouac became the center of media attention. Unlike Ginsberg, Kerouac was constitutionally unsuited to lionization, literary or otherwise. He was a profoundly shy man, as Gerald Nicosia's biography amply demonstrates. Fame also exacerbated Kerouac's alcoholism because drink was the easiest way he knew to toughen his ego enough to resist the prickings of public scrutiny. Kerouac had always been reluctant to perform, passing up an opportunity to be part of the historic Six Gallery affair, and his live readings at the Village Vanguard around Christmas 1957 turned into a drunken debacle. For whatever reasons, Kerouac was unfit for celebrity, yet that lifestyle was suddenly thrust upon him. In part it was Kerouac's celebrity status that made it inevitable for a generation of readers to focus their primary attention on his life, construing his works as pure autobiography, plain and simple. Thus, to approach *Mexico City Blues* by way of its author's life is, if not necessarily the most productive, at least the most predictable way of testing the blood of the poet, and it is far from being an uninteresting way.

When, in July 1955, Kerouac left North Carolina, where he and his mother had been staying at his sister's house, three matters were uppermost in his mind. First was his writing. He had been struggling for over four years to place his most important novel, *On the Road*. The scroll manuscript of the story, written in April 1951, signaled his breakthrough into spontaneous composition, but it had been turned down flat by Robert Giroux, who had edited Kerouac's first novel. Subsequently, Malcolm Cowley, a well-known man of letters of the Lost Generation who worked in the 1950s as an adviser to Viking Press, had become interested in the manuscript. Cowley did much to encourage Kerouac, touting him in essays and arranging for the publication of excerpts from *On the Road*, but it took him several years and a staff change in Viking's editorial board to win acceptance for the novel.

Meanwhile, Kerouac, undaunted, pushed on toward further innovations. *Visions of Cody*, his most experimental book, followed *On the Road* almost immediately. In some ways, it is a version of the first novel. After *Visions of Cody* came *Dr. Sax*, conceived about the same time as the original conventional version of *On the Road*, followed by *Maggie Cassidy* and then *The Subterraneans*, which some critics consider the epitome of Kerouac's spontaneous style. Apparently Kerouac was not only undeterred by his failure to publish, but he also actually pushed himself to great imaginative heights during this period. The cost in strength to his ego was, however, immense. In order to maintain his self-confidence, which forms the basis of any author's authority, he had to continually pump himself up by various means.

At last, in the early summer of 1955, he received some assurance from Cowley that *On the Road* would win acceptance at Viking. Though self-satisfaction should have been the reward of his persistence, Kerouac's response was much more complex. Instead of feeling vindicated, he began to doubt the value of the very instrument of his success: the ego. It was natural, then, when he arrived in Mexico City, to take up in his writing an examination of that elusive and perhaps illusory mental organ.

By this time, an inquiry into the nature of ego also seemed warranted by his study of Buddhism, which had been going on for about a year and a half. Dwight Goddard's *Buddhist Bible*,

Kerouac's primary catechism, emphasized in its selection of scrip-
tures the theme of anatta, the achievement of a state of egoless-
ness. Although Kerouac was not terribly interested in either exis-
tentialism or depth-psychology (with the notable exception of
Reich's theory of orgasm), his inquisition of the ego placed him
in the very mainstream of Postmodern thought.

In spiritual terms the abolition of the ego meant release
from suffering, which Kerouac, in accord with Buddhism, speci-
fied as the essential quality of existence. In personal terms, how-
ever, Kerouac may not have realized the absolute necessity of a
concept of ego for his own worldview. The very autobiographical
content of his writing depends for its coherence on an ego that
connects past and present. In this sense, Kerouac's spontaneous
poetics—an attempt to formalize discontinuity—was partly at
odds with the most dynamic theme of all his work: the relation of
memory to sensuous immediacy. In order to obliterate his ego, it
would have been necessary for Kerouac to detach himself from his
own past, a maneuver he could never accomplish, and one which,
had he been able to accomplish it, would have either saved him as
a person or utterly destroyed him as a writer. His unsuccessful
struggle with the concept of ego may also explain why Kerouac
gave up his active study of Buddhism when he began to achieve
some fame. Drinking helped to bolster his ego; Buddhism served
primarily to diminish it. Nevertheless, at the time he sat down to
write *Mexico City Blues*, his state of mind was probably such that
he could contemplate in good faith transforming his life into a life
without ego. Perhaps it was the intensity of his personal struggle
that enabled him to transmute this theme so effectively into his
poetry.

The third thing on Kerouac's mind as he traveled south that
summer of 1955—along with the complex issues of writing and
Buddhism—was paternity. In January he had been forced into
court by his second wife, Joan Haverty, who had to press charges
repeatedly to exact support payments for their daughter, Jan. Ker-
ouac was typically double-minded about Jan: in public he vehe-
mently denied being her father, but in private he recognized the
striking resemblance of her features to his and admitted, even to
Joan, that she must be his daughter. Although Kerouac's lawyer,

Eugene Brooks (Allen Ginsberg's brother), convinced the New York court that Kerouac's phlebitis had incapacitated him, Kerouac still feared that Joan would continue to hound him. His regular trips to Mexico in the 1950s were at least partly calculated to throw the law off his trail.

Still, the question of fatherhood haunted him in his little adobe hut on the top of the building at 212 Orizaba Street. It elicited some of Kerouac's deepest feelings because it touched on his most dearly held beliefs. Personally, Kerouac was bound by the promise he made to his father on his deathbed to support and care for his mother. Somehow, Kerouac construed this promise exclusively: he could only support one family, and that family was Memere. As a writer he had certainly taken advantage of his mother's care. He wrote several of his novels at night in her apartment while she slept after a hard day's work in the shoe factory. While this bound him even closer to his mother—in fact, it made him her dependent well into adulthood—he found it a workable situation for writing. Unlike his mother, his lovers were not always so tolerant of his demands or understanding of his devotion to his career. Indeed, it was the composition of the scroll version of *On the Road*, as much as anything else, that ended Kerouac's brief marriage to Joan. (See the juxtaposition of the novel and marriage in the "87th Chorus.") Finally, in terms of his interpretation of his newfound Buddhism, Kerouac also rejected paternity in an abstract spiritual sense. (See his argument in the "216th-B Chorus.") If suffering characterizes existence, it must be wrong to bring a child into the world, he reasoned. "Born to die" seemed to him an insufficient motto for fatherhood.

Several other significant features of Kerouac's life also come into play in my reading of *Mexico City Blues*. One is the change in Kerouac's relationship with Neal Cassady, the hero of two of his novels, that is marked by Neal's conspicuous absence from the poem. It is worth recalling here that Allen Ginsberg was composing "Howl," whose "secret hero" is "N.C., cocksman and Adonis of Denver" (14), at the very same time Kerouac was jotting down the two-hundred-odd choruses of *Mexico City Blues*. Ginsberg's friendship with Cassady was of slightly longer standing than was Kerouac's, so it seems remarkable that Ginsberg was just then getting around to according Neal the legendary status that Kerouac had created several years earlier in *On the Road* and *Visions of Cody* (which was originally titled "Visions of Neal"). In fact, Cassady remained virtually ostracized from Kerouac's writing throughout his Buddhist period, reappearing only in *Big Sur*, the drunkard's self-exposé.

A certain defensiveness in the presentation of Buddhism in *Mexico City Blues* also explains Cassady's absence from the poem. At about the same time Kerouac was discovering Buddhism in Asvaghosa's *Acts of the Buddha*, Cassady chanced upon a copy of one of Gina Cerminara's books about the American clairvoyant Edgar Cayce. By the time Kerouac arrived for one of his lengthy visits to the Cassadys in early 1954, both Neal and his wife, Carolyn, were firmly entrenched Cayceites. Understandably, then, especially in the light of Kerouac's Catholic education, his Buddhism took on the tone of apologetics. Much of the discussion of karma and reincarnation in *Mexico City Blues* is, I believe, supposed to be a kind of poetic *coup de grace* to Kerouac's arguments with Cassady on these topics. In a sense, then, Cassady is the invisible antagonist of the poem. (And this is only one of many ways in which *Mexico City Blues* provides a subtext for "Howl," and vice versa. The two poems are thoroughly reversed images of each other, and they can be read most productively as mutual commentary on the poetics of frankness and spontaneity and as arguments for differing tactics for presenting these values.) Cassady's absence is equally conspicuous in *The Dharma Bums*, written two years later, where Kerouac substituted Gary Snyder as his new hero. Cassady was historically on the scene for the events described in that novel, which came toward the end of Kerouac's Buddhist period, but fictional selectivity of another more hostile variety eliminated from the reader's attention an anti-Buddhist figure.

Three family members also assume Cassady's legendary proportions in Kerouac's writing, including in *Mexico City Blues*. The first is Gerard, Kerouac's only brother, who died at the age of nine, when Kerouac was just four. Even before his death, the nuns at Gerard's grade school had unofficially canonized him. After his death, his mother took up the theme of his saintliness. Memere was even known to have expressed the wish, in the heat of anger, that Kerouac instead of Gerard had died. Consequently, while the image of Gerard in the poem represents a distinctly Catholic presence, the modern equivalent of St. Francis (who also plays a prominent role in balancing against the Buddhism in *Mexico City Blues*), on a psychological level the image of Kerouac's brother stands for something much more ambiguous. Kerouac fully revealed the anxiety involved in writing about Gerard when he wrote his novelistic homage to him about six months after the composition of *Mexico City Blues*. In *Visions of Gerard*, a novel like *Tristessa* in which Buddhist and Catholic values merge in a unique Kerouacian spiritual synthesis, the reciprocal relationship between holiness and guilt comes clear.

Kerouac's treatment of his father in the poem is simpler, though much more important dramatically and theologically. Leo provides the image of the "Ignorant Man" ("103rd Chorus"), the embodiment of unsought egolessness in ordinary human behavior. The Oedipal dimensions of the father-son relationship are only too obvious, and Kerouac often treats them playfully, as he did in naming his own character Leo Percepied—"Father Oedipus"—in *The Subterraneans*. Nevertheless, these dimensions do exist. Kerouac was, for instance, the only one present when his father died, so for the rest of his life he bore the main emotional responsibility for Leo's death. His reverence for his father became so extreme that Kerouac seems to have tried—consciously or not—to mold himself into another Leo. I mean this in more than the obvious sense in which he replaced his father as Memere's husband. Photos of Kerouac in the late 1960s are striking because of his bloated appearance and slovenly posture; he had come to resemble his father even physically. More than that, under the influence of heavy drinking he allowed Leo's attitudes, especially his bigotry, to assume control of his personality. Even Kerouac's alcoholism provided a way of emulating his father's failure and miserable death. I find this one of the most astonishing symbolic features of Jack Kerouac's existence, and evidence in *Mexico City Blues* indicates that he consciously planned the pattern of his life to repeat the pattern of his father's life.

Kerouac's mother, Gabrielle, or Memere (meaning something like "granny" in French-Canadian) as she was often called, is usually present on some level in all of his writing. In *Mexico City Blues* she usurps the function of "secret hero" despite the appearance created by the the cluster of choruses devoted to Charlie Parker at the end of the poem. She is identified with Damema, "mother of Buddhas," the wife of the Tibetan sage Milarepa, and even takes on qualities of the Blessed Virgin. For a less autobiographical poet, such an identification would perhaps not be so troubling. For Kerouac, with his sublime ability to raise much of his mental apparatus to the conscious level, it borders on megalomania and certainly calls into serious question his striving toward egolessness. The use Kerouac makes of his mother in the poem is also troubling because it threatens to remove the critical distance we assume is necessary to create symbolic interaction in art. In this respect Kerouac seems to have simply transferred the symbolic dimension from his psyche, and that effect makes the poem—like much of the rest of his writing—easier to psychoanalyze than to criticize. It also bespeaks the possibility of a positive lack of technical control, which, under the rubric of spontaneity, he would have intended.

All three of these family members (to the virtual exclusion of his sister) played important roles in the Duluoz Legend, the Balzacian conception of a saga-structure to encompass and order all of Kerouac's works of fiction. Though there are gaps in the chronology, Kerouac did complete many of the books in his projected legend, which, as it stands, begins with *Visions of Gerard* and ends with *Satori in Paris*. The relation of *Mexico City Blues* to the Duluoz Legend in general is an intriguing one. Since the poem records certain events that happened as it was being written, it falls in one sense into the same category as the first part of the novella, *Tristessa*, which was written in the summer of 1955. Like some of Kerouac's other works, however, the poem reaches from the present back into the distant past, like Proust's fiction, to weave its fabric by combining threads of sensuous immediacy and significant recollection.

But *Mexico City Blues* treats the recollections in a more systematic way: it gathers into a group of choruses (the "87th" to "104th") the kernel of Kerouac's youth, then it touches on various important events in his adult life, and finally it merges with the present to capture the "future memories," so to speak, memories as they are being made. One of my arguments for the importance of the poem hinges on this observation. Since *Mexico City Blues* presents the Duluoz Legend in a nutshell, it must have special significance among Kerouac's works from the point of view of both writer and readers. In this poem, I believe, Kerouac found a way to encapsulate his past, represent it in a symbolic religious dimension, and thus use ego—the product of family, memory, and individual desire—as a means to transcend itself. His family members become figures of legend, and he himself becomes a Tathagata, one who has "passed through," as he calls himself in the "216th-B Chorus," the "Venerable Kerouac."

More than a fourth of the choruses of *Mexico City Blues* contain references to events in Kerouac's life, and this sheer bulk, if nothing else, makes autobiography one of the most important themes in the poem. Beyond that, however, the autobiography in the poem is very carefully developed, with three distinct time frames and a religious significance all its own. The time frames function almost spatially to create perspective: close-up, medium range, and far distance. The religious motif also connects autobiography to the most important theme of the poem, Kerouac's exploration of the concept of anatta, the possibility of annihilating the self. As the singer of the poem delves deep into his past, recalls significant moments in his adult life, and tries to capture experience as it is happening in the present, he learns that the cost of selflessness is the recognition that even memory is an arbitrary conception. For Kerouac, the great rememberer, this must have been a shocking realization.

In the following pages I will discuss the three time frames in reverse chronological order, starting with the narrative present and moving to Kerouac's distant past. The present is embodied in the poem primarily in descriptions of the opinions and activities of Kerouac's neighbor on Orizaba Street, the aging junkie William Maynard Garver. A friend of Burroughs in New York City, Garver earned a reputation on the street as an overcoat thief. Through him Kerouac met Esperanza Villanueva, who became the model for Tristessa, the title character of the novella Kerouac began at the same time he was writing *Mexico City Blues*. Addiction—embodied in Garver's morphine habit—became a governing metaphor for Kerouac at this time, as it had for Burroughs in earlier years. The opiates stand for desire, necessity, and even art; thus, Garver, with his long, rambling monologues that stirred Kerouac's imagination, becomes the muse of the poem. The first of several groups of choruses that deal exclusively with Garver makes this clear. The "33rd Chorus" is laced with quotations I take to be transcriptions of Garver's talk. The old man describes himself as "An explorer of souls / and cities." Like the poet,

> the addict explores
> the world anew
> and creates a world
> in his own image.

The junkie, in unintended parody of the thirty-three-year-old writer, characterizes himself as "an idealist / who has outgrown [his] idealism." Such parallels between muse and poet expand in the course of the poem, so it is no coincidence that Garver's description of his own quest is followed, in the "34th Chorus," by an explanation of his origins. He even relates himself to the politics of Whitman and Kerouac:

> But I'm really a citizen
> of the world
> who hates Communism
> and tolerates Democracy.

After a brief interlude in which the singer generalizes on Garver's junkie philosophy—"No direction to go / (but) / (in) ward" ("36th Chorus")—he returns to the present in the "38th Chorus" to describe a somewhat ludicrous episode in which his companion hammers some tacks with a stone statue, his "Aztec hammer." Simply watching Garver perform his household tasks elicits all sorts of ideas, starting with Cleopatra in the "38th Chorus," proceeding to Beowulf and Frankenstein in the "39th

Chorus," and concluding with Rabelais in the "40th Chorus." The purpose of this section, which also serves to tie Garver to Mexican mythology, seems to be primarily aesthetic. In the "38th Chorus," in the midst of performing his menial task, Garver comments: "It's take an artist / to do all this." The statement relates to Kerouac's spontaneous poetics. What has released the flood of associations in this sequence of choruses is a combination of Garver's talk and the distraction of the poet's attention by his mundane household activity. The decoration of the home, however, turns out to be analogous to the composition of poetry. Typically, Kerouac elevates the mundane and demystifies the poetic. The question Garver asks in the "40th Chorus" to conclude this sequence falls with unexpected weight: "What do you think?" His actions have provided the poet with several moments of rich intuitive association, so the simple request for an opinion about the effect of redecorating becomes a pun involving both the psychology of the poet and the composition of the poem.

In a kind of detached coda, the singer returns to this theme several choruses later when he describes a dream about Garver in the "46th Chorus." In it the singer is wandering mentally as Garver talks about a multitude of topics, including "the crossroads of the world." He brings himself back, only to be startled by the realization that he is

> dreaming
> In beginnings already
> And ending's nowhere
> To be seen
> Yet forgotten—
> Is all.

He has already progressed, with Garver's collaboration, toward a recognition that the past is an illusion of continuity by which the ego asserts its existence, power, and control. The phrase "Is all," which concludes the chorus, proves perfectly ambiguous in this respect. The dream is everything, and everything is dream. But colloquially, it's no big deal. It's just a dream is all.

Though it is apparently Garver's voice that sets off the

"bacon and eggs" routine beginning the "80th Chorus," the next full series of choruses devoted to him (excluding the paired "133rd" and "134th" choruses) does not occur until after the midway point in the poem. Here again, beginning with the "153rd Chorus," the series centers in mundane activity: "Tucking the sheets in / of no consequence." The "rich cover" of the following chorus may be the same one Garver was tacking on in the first sequence (in the "40th Chorus"), and the stanza in which it appears makes an allusion to the boat that is sailing through the poem, the "S.S. Mainline," which is seen in the "229th Chorus" to be "reeling in merit like mad." The mundane, the poetic, and the religious again merge in Garver's room as Kerouac is in the very act of composition. Because of its placement later in the poem, this second sequence takes a distinctly devotional turn. The singer imagines Garver's death, quotes Gerard's assurance that "Everything's all right" (see *Visions of Gerard* 14), and concludes in the "155th Chorus" with an image of reincarnation.

In the "155th Chorus" Kerouac uses a naturalistic image of flies in a bottle to convey his feelings about souls awaiting rebirth. We are already in heaven, which is symbolized by the blueness of the bottle. We "rage & wait," but the result of our waiting is the "Rosy / of Purple O Gate / O J O." I construe this to mean that the womb here is the Tathagata, that is, the completely perfected Buddha, represented by the Orb of Womb mentioned two choruses later. *Ojo*, likewise, is the eye of God. Kerouac, developing his argument with Cassady about rebirth, is suggesting that, like Garver in his morphine dreams, he will be reborn into Nirvana.

The last of the Garver sequences recounts a pair of the junkie's dreams. The first, described in the "162nd" and "163rd" choruses, is set in the Tombs, the old Manhattan jail. Garver has two fantasies of escape, one involving a harem scene and the other a surrealistic process that identifies breathing with growing alternately fat and thin. The second dream is a gruesome one in which Garver and his friends are cooking food on iron plates on the floor of Grand Central Station. Suddenly, he finds himself sitting at a table only to discover that one of his fellow bums is cooking Garver's leg with steam. The interpretation of this second dream comes in Garver's voice, but the religious terminology in which it is couched belongs strictly to Kerouac. The point of the dream-story is that "the essence does not pass / From mouth to mouth," but rather "it's ignorance does. / ignorant form" ("165th Chorus"). The images of confinement (with its corresponding fantasies of escape, including sex and drugs) and pain reinforce the Buddhist theme of the poem by illustrating the double illusion of taking the forms of life too seriously. Garver's dream occurs within the context of the dream of life, as the junkie himself had already pointed out in the "76th Chorus."

It is no accident that the "166th Chorus," the one following the Garver sequence, begins with the phrase—which may be Garver's as well—"A home for unmarried fathers." Amid the welter of associations, Kerouac is trying to work out one of the most serious problems of his life, the paternity of his daughter. In general Kerouac loved children, but he abhorred the idea of bringing them into the world. He had been in court to answer his second's wife's child support suit just six months before he wrote *Mexico City Blues*. Garver's dreams may have served as parables of Kerouac's attempt to justify his denial of paternity on a spiritual level. That "essence does not pass / From mouth to mouth" ("165th Chorus) might even be taken in a restricted autobiographical sense to mean that Kerouac's responsibility for Jan's birth, even her very existence, is just one more illusion. If my reading seems tortured, it is no more contradictory than Kerouac's own double-mindedness about his daughter. His autobiographical meditations in *Mexico City Blues*, as in most of his writing, are filled with similar ambivalence. He senses that he must neutralize the details of his own life in order to escape from the domination of self, but some of the facts are more stubborn than his own memories. Some of the facts have lives of their own.

The issue of paternity also intrudes into the middle time frame of autobiographical choruses, which encompasses the time from Kerouac's first road trip in 1941 (recounted in the "54th Chorus") up to the early 1950s. In the "136th Chorus," for instance, he addresses his first wife, Edie. "Potatoes of paternity / Grow deep," he says, alluding on one level, perhaps, to Edie's abortion in 1942, while Kerouac was sailing to Greenland aboard the SS *Weems*. Potatoes, besides being a necessary part of the sound effects, may also refer to Kerouac's Celtic heritage, and a passage in *Visions of Gerard* connects the *pomme de terre* with Kerouac's father (95). Thus, the issue of his own birth also becomes problematic in these autobiographical passages. As Leo takes on a central role in the poem, Kerouac tries doubly hard to reconcile his new belief that all is illusion, despite the apparently irrefutable contradictory evidence of paternity—his own and his father's.

Three other issues, moreover, share the stage of this middle time frame: work, the literary life, and death. The first topic may be a response to Kerouac's sister Nin's criticism of his way of life, which he quotes in the "201st Chorus": "They think they dont / have to work / because they are God." Nicosia confirms that this was Nin's attitude toward Kerouac in 1955, when he stopped at her farm in North Carolina before heading for Mexico (476), and in the "227th Chorus" Kerouac brings himself to admit his own laziness. In the poem, then, he must remind her—and himself—that he has done regular work for periods of time. He mentions his railroad work in two of the most poignant choruses in *Mexico City Blues*, the "22nd" and the "146th." The power of the latter chorus particularly affected one of Kerouac's biographers, who identifies the locations and reckons the time reference to be fall 1952 (Clark 118). The appearance of laziness in the writer's life worried Kerouac, especially after his father's death in 1946. Since "work" constituted the first of the three elements of the Kerouac family motto, coming before "suffer and love," these choruses form part of his (self-)defense.

Two incidents from his literary career also stuck in his mind, surfacing in several of his books, including *Mexico City Blues*. The first of these involves John Clellon Holmes, a fellow novelist Kerouac met in the late 1940s and remained friends with until his death. Holmes made his mark as the author of the first Beat novel, *Go*, published in 1952 after Kerouac had already written both the scroll version of *On the Road* and *Visions of Cody*. Naturally Kerouac felt that Holmes had stolen his thunder, and to make matters worse, had stolen it by means of a conventional novel that gained him a $20,000 advance for paperback rights. Both McNally (167) and Nicosia (370) give detailed accounts of

Kerouac's jealousy. In the "60th Chorus" the singer presents the issue as one of forgiveness, and though he never expressly forgives Holmes for his "sin," he implies that he does have compassion in the form of "eyes of Avalokitesvara," Kerouac's favorite bodhisattva, or Buddhist saint.

The second significant incident from Kerouac's literary career, which involved novelist Gore Vidal, produces one of the more amusing choruses in the *Mexico City Blues*: the "74th." Nicosia says that Kerouac once actually seduced Vidal, who was already a successful writer by the mid-1950s, to impress Ginsberg and Burroughs (444). Kerouac himself describes the incident, which occurred in the San Remo bar in Greenwich Village during the late summer of 1953, in *The Subterraneans* (71–74). The fictional account omits the sexual aspect of the encounter altogether while the poetic version focuses on it, though with ambiguous results: "Didnt know I was / a Come-Onner, did you? / (Come-on-er)". One way to read this is as an admission that while he did "come on" to Vidal, his real nature is either heterosexual (er = her) or simply one of hesitant confusion (er = speech pause). It may also be that "Come-on-er" is supposed to sound like *commoner*, suggesting that Kerouac may have been daunted by Vidal's sophistication and that he now realizes his actions were rather crude. In any case, this chorus provides a good example of Kerouac's attempt to rework the legend of his life into a much more condensed, and perhaps more honest, record by using the resources of ambiguity available in poetry.

One of the major themes of Kerouac's work as a whole is death, so it comes as no shock that death enters into the autobiographical element of *Mexico City Blues*. In fact, death—in the form of suicide—provides the prelude to the extended series of autobiographical choruses I call the Lowell Canto, which recounts the origins of the Duluoz Legend. Three earlier choruses, however, treat death in different ways.

First, the "47th Chorus" appears to allude to the death of Kerouac's first literary friend, Sammy Sampas, who died in North Africa in 1943. "Where is Italy?" the singer wonders at the beginning of the chorus. A restatement in Buddhist terms follows the question and then a series of horrific images, including a possible allusion to Burroughs's Dr. Benway, who was in the very early stages of imaginative development at this time. The chorus winds down to the singer's own dream of a Japanese boy "sitting on a wall / On Kamikaze Boulevard." This chorus expresses all the guilt and anguish Kerouac felt about the war, first because he could not tolerate the regimentation required to participate in it as a fighting man, and second because he sensed that men like Sampas had been sent off to little more than honorable suicide. Sampas had taught Kerouac the comradeship of literature and inspired his formative early appreciation of the fiction of Thomas Wolfe. Kerouac and Sampas had intended to join the merchant marine together, but Kerouac signed on alone, leaving Sampas to join the Navy as a corpsman. "What happened in Italy?" the singer asks (himself). Among other things, Sammy Sampas received his death wounds at the battle of Anzio. In strict Buddhist terms, the answer should be "nothing," but that would have required Kerouac to detach himself from the most troubling and resonant parts of his past, an act of letting go he was just preparing to perform.

Another pair of choruses, the "55th" and "56th," also concerns death. In the first of these, the singer recounts reading *The Brothers Karamazov* during a hospital stay. According to Nicosia, Kerouac read Dostoevsky's novel during stays in V. A. hospitals for phlebitis in both 1945 and 1951 (161, 355), and though the second hospital, Kingsbridge, looked out on the "rooftops of the Bronx," identifying the chorus with the 1951 episode, the two events are probably conflated on purpose. The classic novel suggests the theme of paternity (which was also associated with phlebitis since that ailment exempted Kerouac from his child support payments in 1955) and, more precisely, the psychology of the father-son relationship and the death of the father. In the "56th Chorus," in fact, the singer muses on his own death "of die-sadness," the Kaiser's death from leukemia, his uncle John's death from diabetes, and finally, the death of an "Old Italian Fruiterer" from Banti's disease. Charters reports that Kerouac's father, in fact, died of Banti's disease (59). Kerouac's phlebitis attacks always made him even more acutely conscious of his own mortality than usual, and given the Buddhist context of the poem and his spiritual concerns about paternity it seems reasonable that he would associate death with fatherhood. The quest for liberation in *Mexico City Blues*, seen here in just one facet of one theme, entails the acceptance of suffering (and by extension of fatherhood and birth) as a means of abandoning the ego and, consequently, escaping death. This became an exceedingly difficult and complex struggle for Kerouac, who was restricted both by his devotion to his father and by his pride in his own memory.

The tightest linkage of choruses in *Mexico City Blues*—the Lowell Canto, which includes the "87th" to "104th" choruses— uses autobiography to bring immense dramatic tension to the poem. The Lowell Canto represents the third and most difficult time frame, the distant past. Though Kerouac was not an existentialist, the dilemma posed in this section of the poem is an existential dilemma: If one chooses to live, how can one dispel the debilitating illusion of one's past in order to live fully in the present? The prelude to the Lowell Canto, which I call the Suicide Prelude (the "79th" to "86th" choruses), itself begins with a question: "Story About What?" The singer answers (himself) that the story is about both "Babyhood" and suicide. It is difficult to tell for certain, but the voice of the other character in the prelude sounds like Garver's. Because Garver is the muse of the poem, his instructions here would carry even more weight.

He is making breakfast in the "80th Chorus." His advice to the singer is to "stop / writing poetry / And dig in." That is, he should live in the present instead of the past. Almost immediately, the musical theme of "Harvest Moon" begins to develop out of another romantic song. The association is obscure, but Kerouac may have associated the tune with madness because of an incident that occurred while he was incarcerated in the mental ward at Newport Naval Station in December 1942 (Nicosia 104). The singer's ability to answer the larger question about suicide, in other words, is thwarted by his suspicion that he is mentally incompetent to decide. The Suicide Prelude ends with the repeated admonition (like something straight out of Camus): "Take your pick." As a Catholic, Kerouac considered suicide a sin, but at the outset of this intense autobiographical revery he cannot resist imagining what life would have been like if he had never lived it. This hypothetical fallacy constitutes one image of egolessness in the poem, madness another.

The Lowell Canto begins with a reference to *On the Road,* the experimental text that was so much on Kerouac's mind when he went to Mexico in 1955. The scroll version of this novel was composed during Kerouac's brief second marriage, and may in fact have contributed to the breakup; thus, the mention of it, which seems spontaneous, predictably calls up a recollection of Kerouac's second wife and the romantic illusion he associated with her. In addition, the reference to *On the Road* must have caused a recollection of Neal Cassady, although Cassady is not mentioned specifically here or anywhere else in the poem. The energy released by Kerouac's associations with *On the Road* produces a kind of surreal explosion, which includes a phantom that could have come from *Paterson,* as well as a list of imaginary kings, one of whom is literally named "Power." At last the "87th Chorus" calms down into a statement of mission: "Make it a great story & confession / Of all the crazy people you've known / Since early Nineteen Fifty One." It is difficult to tell whether the singer intends for this mission to apply to the poem or to some work of fiction yet to be written. The word "confession," however, recalls Spengler's belief that all great writing is subjective revelation of one individual's life, just as it presages the school of poetry that was taking shape in America about this time, the Confessional poets. Neither *On the Road* nor the Lowell Canto, however, deals with events that occurred after 1951.

Rather, in this section of *Mexico City Blues,* Kerouac combines his retelling of his own origins with the themes of romance, madness, and illusion. After proposing a possible first sentence for his autobiography, the singer abandons the project in disgust, calling it a pretentious piece of "golden litteratur" ("88th Chorus"). He resolves to return to the very beginning of his life, and he discovers by recalling his early quest for identity that "I was the first crazy person / I'd known" ("87th Chorus"). This return to his childhood allows Kerouac to avoid discussing Cassady or his pending paternity suit, though it sets him irreversibly on the trail to the source of the illusion of his own life, ultimately the issue of his own paternity.

Almost immediately, he returns (in the "89th Chorus") to his own conception and birth. In a very early chorus (the "19th"), the singer had described Gerard's baptism, which occurred three years before Kerouac was born. He has his origins covered even beyond his own memory, but the upshot of his birth is fear. This fear, the singer believes, could have been eliminated "if somebody coulda told me / it was unreal." Both romance and madness are forms of illusion, so the singer, realizing this, must distinguish between these forms and the essential illusion that is life, as propounded by Buddhism. He confronts the double illusion that is reinforced later in Garver's dreams. To help accomplish the distinction between the two levels of illusion, Kerouac picks up the *oo* sound—Kerouac's favorite sound, judging from his recordings—from "Harvest Moon," the song that implies both romance and madness. The "89th Chorus" (which may also represent a humorous response to Ginsberg's "Howl") ends: "Wild howl Lupine Cold the Moony / and Loony nights." Lupine, besides meaning wolf-like, was the name of the street on which Kerouac was born. It may also refer to his brother Gerard, whose family nickname was Ti Loup, Little Wolf. By means of sound the singer invests these lines with a howling onomatopoeia, redolent of movie werewolves and winter wind, which is yet somehow pleasant to the ear. The *oo* of "Lupine," "Moony," and "Loony" becomes a big bubble blown by the singer's lips—mere words—certainly nothing to be feared.

The next two choruses give the details of young Jackie's premonition of the unreality of things. If the phantom of Gerard was real, all he had to do was endure its attack, "suffer & die" ("91st Chorus"). If it was unreal, then perhaps it really was Gerard. This oscillation between the real and the unreal (in terms of phantoms, no less), like the subsequent account of Garver's dreams, is too much for the rational mind to bear, and so the "91st Chorus" turns into a kind of Zen *koan*. The event you expect "never happens, / Pow!" The difficulty in thinking about illusion practically solves the problem: it is so easy to play games in language with the forms of reality that its true essence must be illusion.

This train of thought begins with the image of a toy house and people in the "92nd Chorus"—the only place in the poem where Kerouac mentions his sister Caroline by name—and concludes with the confirmation of this childhood premonition in a paraphrase of the Lankavatara Sutra (the longest of Kerouac's three favorite Buddhist scriptures) in the "93rd Chorus." This paraphrase also contains an important warning about the false illusion of madness (as opposed to the essential illusion of life): "dont tip, / lose balance, see reality / in images like cardboard." The singer is now ready to begin again by restating the mission, to "describe / The crazy people I've known" ("94th Chorus"). This time the memory involves being taken by his mother to a Lowell tenement, itself "a crazy place." Still, it was perhaps there as a very small child that Kerouac began to perceive in the welter of language that "it's easy to go crazy." From this perception of the illusion of madness springs an insight: "I go crazy sometimes." What follows has ramifications for both the Lowell Canto and the entire autobiographical theme:

> Can't get on with my story,
> write it in verse.
>> Worse
> Aint go no story, just verse.

The whole mission, to write a big confession, resolves itself into the sound of poetry at the moment he internalizes the true nature of illusion. At this moment Kerouac has no story—no autobiography—only the sound of words.

The message brought by Gerard's phantom in the "91st Chorus" is the opposite of the one enunciated by Gerard after his vision (recounted in the "19th Chorus" and in *Visions of Gerard* 65). Instead of "Everything will be alright," it is "Bone / the Brother-Crash." The phantom's message of death leads to the breakthrough in the Lowell Canto. The singer immediately recognizes in the remembered action of playing with cardboard soldiers the same moral as the Lankavatara Sutra: do not "see reality / in images like cardboard /—nor in the brown light of this very kitchen" ("93rd Chorus"). The meaning of death is intermingled

in acts of memory, and the recognition of the illusion in one
brings a recognition of the illusion of the other. The recollection
in the "96th Chorus" leads to a hypothetical fallacy: What if
Jackie had died riding his tricycle as a kid? He would not have
had to witness the death of his loved ones. As it is, death seems
only too real, and thus it presents a serious stumbling block to his
meditations. "I saw my father die, / I saw my brother die," the
singer intones. Then, oddly, though Kerouac preceded his mother
in death: "I saw my mother die / my mother my mother my
mother / inside me." It is as though, in giving birth to his moth-
er's death—and only by doing so—he comes to know intimately
that even death is an illusion.

The remaining choruses in the Lowell Canto focus on Ker-
ouac's father. Gerard has already been sainted; his function in
Kerouac's life is clear; he embodies the time frame of distant past.
Memere, on the other hand, is still alive; her death remains a pro-
jection; she signifies the present. Leo lies in the middle-distance;
the memory of his death bears a heavy freight of guilt; he stands
for the period of Kerouac's early adulthood. Perhaps in imitation
of Gerard, who was sainted by the nuns in Lowell even before his
death, Kerouac chooses apotheosis as the means to reconcile his
relationship with his father. After showing the reader Leo's recip-
rocal awareness of his second son's inevitable death in the "97th
Chorus"—" 'And my poor lil Ti Pousse,' / he thinks of me, / 'He'll
get it too' "—the singer puts this thought in the father's head:
"Wish I was God" ("98th Chorus"). That he worries about his
son's sexuality in the same chorus ("hates to see me / flash sher-
oot") gives some preliminary indication that Leo will come to
stand for more than a spiritual renunciation of the fear of death.
Kerouac is headed toward a synthesis that is unabashedly self-
serving.

At the close of the "99th Chorus," one sees Leo checking
the box for mail in 1924 "looking in the void for nothing." His
life, it appears, has prefigured that of his writer son, who has
grown up to "re-double / the image, in words," an activity of du-
bious value in terms of piercing through illusion to annihilate the
ego. "Simplificus," the name Kerouac gives himself in this absurd
account of his infancy, discovers that while movies recreate the

child's sense of reality, it's still "a blow the baby be" ("101st Chorus"). He wishes the movie would never end, but it does, despite what "the optimists / of holy old religion" say. The Tathagata, as the singer recites, insists that "nothing / is really / born nor dies." The illusion of birth and death, he argues in the "102nd Chorus," depends entirely on "Ignorance": the lack of knowledge of the true essence of reality.

The climax and resolution of the Lowell Canto's dilemma of self comes in the "103rd Chorus." In the first image in this chorus, Leo, a printer by trade, appears "like a shadow / Of ink black," suggesting that the singer associates the foregoing memories with writing, as Kerouac certainly did, but that there is also something deceptive about the vividness of those memories. The description of the dream that follows has an effect similar to the apparition of the phantom of Gerard: the dream is more real—in terms of illusion—than the memory. In the dream, the singer has learned to regard Leo as "the image of Ignorant Man." Three lines, drunkenly indented, connect this image with Kerouac's alcoholism: liquor fortifies the illusion of self and gives one the courage to face death.

The second stanza begins by asserting that death is the constant in the Spenglerian cycle of culture and civilization, an assertion developed later in the "204th Chorus." Its purpose is, I believe, to draw an analogy between the lives of Leo and Kerouac. The singer's growing realization at this point forces him to grant that no death differs in essence from any other death. Finally, he concludes:

> My remembrance of my father
>   in downtown Lowell
>   walking like cardboard cut
>   across the lost lights
>   is the same empty material
>   as my father in the grave.

The gist of the chorus is that Leo in life, Leo in death, Leo in memory, and Leo as an image in the poem are all perfectly arbi-

trary conceptions, exhibiting form but lacking substance. Leo is
the embodiment of Ignorant Man partly because he knew death
even though he was unenlightened, partly because he is now dead,
partly because he exists only in his son's memory, and partly be-
cause he has become part of the Duluoz Legend. By multiplying
the dimensions of Leo's existence, Kerouac stresses how obvious
the illusion of reality becomes when it is examined.

One further meaning of Ignorant Man is also extremely perti-
nent. If essence, as the singer says in interpreting Garver's dreams,
does not pass from mouth to mouth, but rather ignorance does,
then Kerouac's father has fathered him anew in *Mexico City Blues*.
Leo may have also engendered in his son a belief in the illusion of fa-
therhood. This implication is borne out by a later chorus, the
"160th," which is entirely devoted to a stale joke told by Kerouac's
father, a joke the singer turns into the "perfect pome." The joke is
simple. What's another word for future? Answer: come. The di-
lemma of paternity makes its appearance with gruesome clarity, in-
volving as it does a vivid reference to the *vagina dentata*, here per-
haps a metaphor for Joan Haverty's child support lawsuit. But Leo,
the image of Ignorant Man, now speaks as oracle. His joke repre-
sents a moment in life that can be transcribed verbatim into verse. Il-
lusion crosses easily from the medium of life into the medium of lit-
erature. Paternity, it follows, is similarly illusory.

Just as the singer had earlier given birth to his mother's
death, he now prepares to bury his father in his womb. "What's
been buried inside me / for sure?" he asks. "The substance of my
own father's / empty light" ("204th Chorus"). Kerouac has utterly
transformed his own heritage. Singing in the voice of a Postmod-
ern Huckleberry Finn, he winds up the theme of paternity in the
"208th Chorus." After describing Leo's death in an even, narrative
tone—"I've seen them die in chairs / Quietly in cities they never
planned"—he takes on the character of a debauched interlocutor:
"Shoot the sperm cup to me, Jim." This may sound like sheer bra-
vado, but the singer has convinced himself of the reality of illu-
sion. His address to Huck's companion is also a self-thrust jibe.
(Charlie Parker was known to use the name Jim in addressing
people he didn't like [Reisner 116].) He finishes in this way:

> These partitioned Anglo Spanese
> Singing sneerers perturbing
> You in the background
> Are your father's kindly
> buriers.

These lines have two complementary meanings: first, that Leo be-
longed to the Spenglerian fellaheen, and that they, living "as
though the city existed not," are responsible for "perturbing" the
singer of the poem—that is, dispelling his arbitrary conceptions
about the value of his own verse; second, that the "sperm cup" of
paternity has no substance, so there can be no danger in drinking
from it.

While it takes the singer many difficult choruses to establish
the meaning of Leo's mythic status in the poem, the role of the
mother is determined easily—predetermined, one might say. In
the "149th Chorus" the singer expresses his continuing romance
with his mother, who stands in a "doll-like way" just "waiting to
serve" him. In the final stanza, he envisions himself an Indian, one
of the fellaheen himself, "Smoking Hashi / In old Cabashy / By
the Lamp." The "237th Chorus," though less direct, is hardly less
startling. It begins with a French proverb that contains a pun on
Gabrielle Kerouac's nickname. "My mother, you are the earth," it
says literally. But the meaning, as unfolded by the singer, is en-
tirely religious. Mother has little to do with memory and every-
thing to do with spirituality. She brings to mind Damema, and
Damema is like the Virgin Mary (a comparison Kerouac also
makes in *Tristessa* [30]) and Maya, Buddha's natural mother, who

> Died at his childbirth,
> Like all mothers should be,
> going to heaven on their impulse
> Pure and free and champion of birth.

The implication here that the singer himself—whether identified
with Jack Kerouac or not—has been reborn a buddha seems ines-
capable. Maternity presents no problem in the poem, and Memere
is easily transmogrified into a deity. The relative ease of this trans-

formation and her identification with instances of virgin birth help reinforce the case against paternity.

Besides acquitting Kerouac of his presumed responsibility for supporting his daughter, the apotheosis of Gerard, Leo, and Memere into a holy family has a genuine religious intent. Gerard and Memere represent the distant past and the immediate present. Each is fused with the drama of the poem with little difficulty. Only Leo's apotheosis costs the singer considerable effort because he represents the difficult middle ground of Kerouac's life, the part associated with the beginning of his writing career. If Kerouac wanted to escape paternity, he also wanted to avoid fame, and that is why I include the "104th Chorus" in the Lowell Canto. Its first line, "I'd rather be thin than famous," rephrases the opening line of the "64th Chorus": "I'd rather die than be famous." In the earlier chorus, fame is perceived to stand in the way of enlightenment. In the latter, the singer implies that he is already famous, or, as he prophesies in the "179th Chorus," "the most beautiful / Boy of my generation." I think that Kerouac's battle with paternity was, on a less selfish level, a battle against the ego that drove his writing. By transforming himself he hoped to escape from the prison of death and the pitfall of celebrity. The connection with the images fat and thin in Garver's dream is unmistakeable. This is spirituality at its most fundamental level. Kerouac is going about the business of trying to save himself.

One final word in this regard. The metamorphosis of autobiography into religion has the effect of universalizing the theme and the poem. Every family *is* the Holy Family, especially in the Buddhist context. Whether Kerouac believed in Freudian analysis or not, his deployment of the Oedipal model is impeccable, and his feel for the connection between religion and the psyche runs as deep as Freud's. In a pair of early choruses, the "69th" and "70th," he prefigures the transformation the singer will accomplish in the autobiographical theme:

> Who *is* my father?
> Who is my mother?
> Who is my brother?
> Who is my sister?

> I say you're all my father
> > all my mother
> > all my sister
> > all my brother.

What makes *Mexico City Blues* such a remarkable religious poem is
its Christlike gesture, its Buddhalike gesture, of presenting itself as
the story of every human being. Ultimately, Kerouac wishes to es-
cape paternity in the way of the great figures of religion, by ac-
cepting his relationship to all people and assuming responsibility
for the human family. As a thoroughly Postmodern man, how-
ever, he takes it for granted that responsibility is best demon-
strated by a relentless exploration of his own soul. His original
motives were highly personal, indeed self-serving, but he trans-
forms them into a thing of value for us all. In *Mexico City Blues*,
especially in the theme of autobiography, the subjective—as
Spengler prescribed—becomes objective.

4

Kerouac in Mexico, Mexico in Kerouac

[In Mexican history] we are sounding out the last necessities of life itself.
We are learning out of another life-course to know ourselves what we are,
what we must be, what we shall be. It is the great school of our future.

In the "Passing Through" sections of *Desolation Angels*, the
narrator, Duluoz, discusses the conflict he feels between soli-
tude and "the world's action" and describes the geographical
polarities that both symbolize and contain the conflict: "It's only
in Mexico, in the sweetness and innocence, birth and death seem
at all worthwhile" (222). Duluoz's recollection of his impression
of the city also balances the conflicting elements in a charming
equipoise: "Candlelight in a lonely room, and writing about the
world" (222). This dualism is typical of Kerouac's attitude toward
Mexico, and the image and theme of Mexico run through all of
his work, play a major role in *Mexico City Blues* beyond the title
itself, and tie his writing securely to a tradition of European litera-
ture that was taken up with great enthusiasm by the Beats.

Allen Ginsberg, for instance, anticipating his departure for
Mexico City—where he, Gregory Corso, and Peter and Lafcadio
Orlovsky planned to rendezvous with Jack Kerouac in the fall of

1956—sat down to write a poem. "Ready to Roll" identifies the main attractions of life south of the border: the immediate adventure of travel, the low cost of living, escape from repressive authority, abundant drugs, easy and uninhibited sex, an interesting ancient culture, and solitude. Mexico City, the seat of both Native American and Spanish cultures, had already become, in Ginsberg's eyes, "a naked hipster labyrinth," exotic and alluring, hospitable to Beat ideals. From the time of William S. Burroughs's escape over the border from New Orleans after a drug bust in late 1949, Mexico had become both a sanctuary and a site of pilgrimage for Beat writers, and it has continued to fulfill these functions for neo-Beat artists as well. For Kerouac the country satisfied all the needs Ginsberg pointed out and more: it served as a vantage point from which he could observe the frantic doings of the civilized world and provided a garret in which Kerouac could write in peace. Using his prodigious synthetic powers, Kerouac fused the varied significance Mexico held for his contemporaries with his own sense of it in *Mexico City Blues*.

In an impressive and durable work of scholarship called *American and British Writers in Mexico, 1556–1973*, Drewey Wayne Gunn has divided the appeal of Mexico for writers through the centuries into five categories: the possibility of making a fresh start in a strange new country; the thrill of danger in a more violent and lawless setting; isolation, both positive and negative; interest in an unindustrialized culture; and the beauty of Mexican arts (x–xi). In the next-to-last chapter, "The Beat Trail to Mexico," Gunn notes that Beat writers were lured south of the border for all these reasons, but that they are distinguished from other writers because "they formed the only noteworthy group to have worked together in Mexico" (229). Naturally, he places Kerouac squarely within this subcategory of a very special literary tradition. He also believes that the Beats' interest in Mexican primitivism ran deeper, and he observes that many Beat writers went on from Mexico to explore cultures even more remote from America.

The way Beat writers combined the practical and metaphoric values of the country and city of Mexico differs from the way members of the Lost Generation combined those same values of the city of Paris. Burroughs, for instance, the first of the Beats to discover the delights of Mexico, developed an early interest in the Mayan codices (ancient mythological annals), an interest he transmitted to Ginsberg, Kerouac, and other members of their circle at Columbia in the mid-1940s. Near the end of the same decade, however, Mexico took on a much more practical importance for Burroughs: he sought refuge there from narcotics charges stemming from his arrest in New Orleans, an episode described in detail in his novel *Junky*. And in a much later retrospective prologue to the sequel of that novel, titled *Queer*, which is set almost entirely in Mexico City, Burroughs also gives his version of the attractions of the place:

> In 1949, it was a cheap place to live, with a large foreign colony, fabulous whorehouses and restaurants, cockfights and bullfights, and every conceivable diversion. A single man could live well there for two dollars a day. (v)

In short order after his arrival, Burroughs had scored morphine, boys, and guns, his three main addictions, and after a year in the city, he felt like a resident welcoming newcomers and showing them the ropes. "Refugee hipsters," observes the Burroughs character in *Junky*, "trickled down into Mexico" (143). Burroughs's friend Jack Kerouac was chief among these refugees.

The appeal of Mexico for writers influenced by the Beats continued into the 1960s and 1970s. More than half of Ken Kesey's *Garage Sale*, for example, is devoted to a "multi-dimensional screenplay" called "Over the Border," which responds in a farcical way to the Mexico chapters of Tom Wolfe's *Electric Kool-Aid Acid Test*. The similarity of Kesey's flight to Mexico to avoid prosecution for possession of marijuana to Burroughs's earlier escape from U.S. authorities is one of the more obvious symbolic repetitions in American literary history.

Kesey provided another look at Mexico in *Demon Box*, which contains a chapter that satirizes the "Ugly American" from the point of view of one who has enjoyed—and continues to enjoy—Mexican culture on a deeper level. The most poignant chapter of *Demon Box*, however, memorializes the day on which the news arrived of the death of Neal Cassady, who fell unconscious on Mexican railroad tracks, the victim of a combination of *pulque* (cactus wine) and Seconals, just four days short of his forty-fourth birthday, 4 February 1968.

Jan Kerouac, the daughter Kerouac denied, has likewise consciously imitated her father's impulse to seek both experience and refuge in Mexico. She even made her own initial pilgrimage official by visiting her father beforehand in Lowell—her second and final meeting with him. In a scene that should be charged with emotion but that comes off as one of the flattest in *Baby Driver*, Kerouac tells his daughter: "You go to Mexico an' write a book. You can use my name" (259). The irony of his injunction is almost as horrifying as the stillbirth of Jan's own daughter in a Mexican jungle, an event she describes near the outset of the novel her father encouraged her to write. *Trainsong*, her second novel, includes the author's recollection of Kerouac's equally ironic words to his second wife, Joan Haverty, Jan's mother: "Hey, I can't take care of a kid. I gotta write this book" (66). The book he was referring to was, of course, *On the Road*, which culminates in Dean and Sal's two-thousand-mile drive from Denver to Mexico City.

Kerouac's biographers record that he visited Mexico eight times, first in 1950—the trip described in *On the Road*—and last in 1961. These visits, which never lasted more than a couple of months, produced much fine writing. The period they bound marks Kerouac's glory days as a writer, but the circumstances of his stays were always less romantic than the magic envisioned by Sal Paradise. Nevertheless, in Mexico City he managed to transmute the suffering that he believed characterizes all human life into durable works of art with the aid of the special citified isolation provided by his rooftop adobe dwelling at 212 Orizaba Street.

The 1950s was Kerouac's only great decade as a writer, and his first visit to Mexico was partly prompted by disappointing reviews of *The Town and the City*, his first published novel, and his rage at the editorial changes he felt had weakened his prose in that book (Clark 88). He appears to have written little on this first visit, but within three months after his return to the States he had married a woman he barely knew—Joan Haverty—and within the year he produced the spontaneous 175,000-word scroll version of *On the Road*. By this time, Joan, already pregnant, had also kicked him out of their loft apartment.

In early 1952, about two months after the birth of Jan Kerouac and immediately following the completion of the manuscript that ultimately became *Visions of Cody*, Kerouac rode down to Nogales with Neal and Carolyn Cassady. He had just begun an affair with Carolyn, with Neal's knowledge, consent, and encouragement. To complicate matters in his own mind, Kerouac seriously feared that his wife would attempt to track him down to collect child support. Freighted with the conflicting emotions of the previous few months, he fled to Burroughs's apartment in Mexico City, where he soon set to work on *Dr. Sax*—which he had actually begun in the late 1940s—a fusion of memoir and Gothic romance, his contribution of a third part to Goethe's Faust drama. Burroughs, then fighting possible indictment for shooting his wife, a tragedy of Beat lore closely associated with bohemian life in Mexico, was paranoid about Kerouac's dope smoking, and his fears forced Kerouac to smoke and write in the hall bathroom. Still, Kerouac completed a new draft of the novel in a month, incorporating into its Lowell setting the Aztec myth of a cosmic battle between the eagle and the snake.

Near the end of this second stay, Kerouac, suffering utter penury, hatched a fanciful plan to live in the Mexican desert, completely isolated and completely free. But instead he returned to the States, eventually to California, where he wrote "The Railroad Earth" (*Lonesome Traveler* 37–83). When his job on the Southern Pacific petered out, he decided to return to Mexico again. He stopped on the way to try to convince Carolyn Cassady to go with him. Neal objected, and in order to stall his wife's decision, he offered to drive Kerouac to Mexico City himself, scoring marijuana in the process. Realizing that Jack's plans were little more than a pipe dream, Carolyn chose to stay at home while the men set out for the border. Burroughs, meanwhile, had jumped bail and fled further south, and Kerouac, increasingly worried about his nonsupport of his daughter, advised friends to address letters to him under an assumed name. With Burroughs gone, however, loneliness soon set in and forced Kerouac to seek haven in his mother's apartment in Richmond Hill, New York.

In three days in 1953, under the influence of Dostoevsky, Reich, and benzedrine, Kerouac wrote *The Subterraneans*, which epitomizes his spontaneous prose method. Early the following year, he discovered Buddhism through Asvaghosa's *Acts of the Buddha*. The newfound doctrines and terminology galvanized his belief about the centrality of suffering in life and gave him a system within which to express his belief more fully. His spontaneous writing, he thought, also corresponded to the Buddhist descriptions of a spiritually well-trained mind. He felt as well that his newfound religion, like his mother's devotions to the "little way" of St. Therese of Lisieux, was a fellaheen religion. It would require of him much needed self-discipline and isolation. He began to make plans to practice his newfound faith in the Mexican desert (Clark 135).

While his agent, Sterling Lord, and his editor, Malcolm Cowley, worked toward an agreement to publish the sprawling *On the Road*, Kerouac's problems with paternity reached a crisis. In December 1954 he was served with a warrant for nonsupport, and in January he appeared in court prepared to go to jail. His chronic phlebitis, brought on by abuse of amphetamines, caused the case to be suspended for a year, however. That year and the one following—1955 and 1956—constituted the period during which Kerouac took his most important trips to Mexico City.

In the spring of 1955, at his sister's house in North Carolina, Kerouac produced two religious texts, *Buddha Tells Us*, his version of the Surangama Sutra, and *Wake Up*, a brief biography of the Buddha. Also, "The Mexican Girl" episode of fellaheen romance and field labor excerpted by Cowley from *On the Road* appeared in *The Paris Review*. With these successes in the immediate background, Kerouac left in July for Mexico City, where in the next two months he composed the first part of *Tristessa* and all 242 choruses of *Mexico City Blues*.

When Kerouac took possession of an old rooftop adobe dwelling at 212 Orizaba, the first person he met was William Maynard "Bill" Garver, who was living in the ground floor apartment formerly occupied by Burroughs. Garver, under the name

Bill Gains, had played a lead role in Burroughs's hard-boiled depiction of the addict's life in *Junky*. He was the original *hombre invisible*, in whom Burroughs saw a reflection of himself:

> Bill Gains came from a "good family". . . . He was not merely negative. He was positively invisible; a vague respectable presence . . . Gains had a malicious childlike smile that formed a shocking contrast to his eyes which were pale blue, lifeless and old. (41–42)

To this character Kerouac attached himself as scribe and errand boy. His transcriptions of Garver's endless junk monologues provided one strong impetus for the composition of *Mexico City Blues*. Running to make dope connections introduced him to Esperanza, whom he transformed into Tristessa.

The novella named for her is the work with the clearest affinity to *Mexico City Blues*. That it was written in two parts during successive summers underscores the radical division in Kerouac's consciousness, his typical practice being the rapid, uninterrupted composition of an entire story. He attempted to resolve some of his conflicts by having a love affair with Esperanza, but he succeeded only in artistic resolution of them in the novel and poem he wrote from the experiences of that summer. Following Burroughs's literary lead—which was reinforced by the presence of Garver—he turned Esperanza's morphine habit into a metaphor for human need. Esperanza's devotion to the Blessed Virgin also reminded him of his mother's veneration of St. Therese and mirrored his current passion for Buddhism. Her lifestyle corresponded with the bohemian folkways of the East Village and North Beach. The theme of the book is pointed up by Kerouac's usual deft touch at naming characters: real-life Hope becomes fictional Sadness, expressing in a simple reversal his projection of the fellaheen worldview and imposing on it an Oriental reconciliation of opposites.

In the second part of *Tristessa*, written in 1956, the narrator, having returned to Mexico after "a four thousand mile voyage from the mountain peak near Canada," remarks on his experience of the previous year:

> I wrote poems in [Garver's] room all last summer when
> Tristessa was *mine, mine*, and I wouldn't take her—I had some
> silly ascetic or celibacious notion that I must not touch a
> woman—My touch might have saved her—
> Now too late—. (65)

Kerouac's understanding of Buddhist doctrine and self-discipline
had apparently given way to an impulse toward salvation through
sex. More than Kerouac's backsliding, however, this passage repre-
sents a cockeyed but intelligible application of Pauline dogma re-
garding sex. The changes wrought on Kerouac during the fall of
1955 and the spring and summer of 1956 were sufficient to ex-
plain this shift of values. Not only was it a year of intense per-
sonal and artistic experiment for Kerouac, but it was also the year
in which the Beats took shape as a literary movement in the eyes
of the public.

When Kerouac arrived fresh from Mexico to stay with him
in Berkeley, Allen Ginsberg had already finished the first draft of
"Howl." Ginsberg and Kerouac had discussed the poem by mail,
and there are several direct references to its title in *Mexico City
Blues*. Ginsberg, by the same token, had adapted Kerouac's
method of spontaneous writing, with jazz as its main aesthetic
source and model, to the vatic utterance of "Howl." At the revo-
lutionary Six Gallery reading on 7 October 1955, Kerouac cheer-
led the audience as Ginsberg stole the show. In *On the Road*,
written more than four years earlier, Dean and Sal have a pro-
phetic vision of the Ginsberg character, Carlo Marx, in the role of
a bop tenorman in a San Francisco nightclub who "blew two hun-
dred choruses of blues, each one more frantic than the other, and
no signs of failing energy" (167). In this fateful twist, Kerouac
cast himself as part of the audience for the poem he himself would
later write. Historically, Ginsberg was speaking for both of them
in 1955 as he read "Howl," and the triumph of his poem was also
a triumph for its unperformed counterpart, *Mexico City Blues*.

During this same period Kerouac befriended Gary Snyder,
who by virtue of his backwoods origin and experience, his anthro-
pological knowledge of Native American cultures, and his study
and practice of Buddhist doctrine, swiftly and conveniently re-

placed Neal Cassady as Kerouac's exemplar. A backpacking trip with Snyder provided some of the material for *The Dharma Bums*, and Kerouac's job as a fire lookout the following summer, which was made possible by Snyder's recommendation, provided the rest. In January 1956, back at his sister's home in North Carolina awaiting confirmation of the Forest Service job, Kerouac wrote *Visions of Gerard*, a prose elegy for his older brother. Later, after hitchhiking back to California to stay with Snyder in a cabin in Marin County, Kerouac also wrote *The Scripture of the Golden Eternity*, his American sutra, and *Old Angel Midnight*, a creation story in the style of *Finnegans Wake*. Kerouac's Buddhist studies led him to the extremes of literary innovation. He was willing, at this point, to risk both convention and meaning in order to express himself.

When Kerouac's fire lookout job began in late June, the stage was set for a profound experience of some sort. As it turned out, nine weeks on a mountain top was more isolation than Kerouac's sociable personality could stand. He nearly lost his mind. Uncomfortable as he was with the temptations of society and desirous as he was of a chance to practice meditation and self-discipline, the solitary confinement of Desolation Peak reduced Kerouac to a state of abject paranoia. Instinctively, his thoughts turned "south in the direction of my intended loving arms of senoritas" (*Desolation Angels* 7). By his last day on the job, only his beat shoes and heavy pack prevented him from literally running down the mountain. Still, after stopovers in Seattle and San Francisco, he headed back to the Mexico City "and a resumption of my solitude in a hovel in the city" (*Desolation Angels* 219). But there was solitude and there was solitude. The momentum of Kerouac's descent from Desolation Peak carried him back to a more productive isolation, only two stories up, and his rooftop dwelling on Orizaba Street came to represent the definitive contrast and artistic counterpoint to the stark shack on the mountainside. This counterpoint makes *Desolation Angels*, which begins with the same incidents covered in the second half of *The Dharma Bums*, a most powerful fictional memoir.

Though he sat down almost immediately to begin writing Book I of *Desolation Angels* by candlelight, Kerouac could not bring himself to write the second half until 1961, five years later. Perhaps the memories were too painful or chaotic, or perhaps the fame that ensued from the publication of *On the Road* in 1957 simply interposed. In any case, the halves of that novel, like the halves of *Tristessa*, which he was also working to complete, graphically represent Kerouac's divided consciousness. A sympathetic reading of *Desolation Angels* is essential for a thorough understanding of the value of Mexico in his writing, a value the book's narrator characterizes in this way:

> MEXICO—A GREAT CITY FOR THE ARTIST, where he can get cheap lodgings, good food, lots of fun on Saturday nights (including girls for hire)—where he can stroll the streets and boulevards unimpeded and for that matter at all hours of the night while sweet little policemen look away minding their own business which is crime prevention and detection. (221)

This explanation, romantic as it sounds, squares perfectly with those of Gunn and of the other Beat writers. In Mexico Kerouac's artistic activity—he painted and sketched there, too—was spurred by his sense of a benign fellaheen society: its sensuality, its vices, its religion, its spirit.

Desolation Angels also explains the specific attraction Kerouac had to Bill Garver (who was called Bull Gaines in this work and in *Tristessa*): "The dope fiend and the artist," Gaines says, "have lots in common" (229). To discover precisely what qualities the two professions shared, Kerouac had conceived, in the previous summer of 1955, the idea of turning Garver's learned monologues into poems. For his part, Bill, who had often served as prison librarian during his sentences for theft convictions, had acquired a wide, free-ranging learning. Junk made him voluble, and his discourse provided a program of ideas and a confessional atmosphere for Kerouac's poetic investigation of the psyche. Kerouac's study of Buddhism combined with Garver's eclectic knowledge to make the resolution of conflicts about religion, identity, writing, evil, and a host of other matters seem eminently possible. This potential for reconciliation—and thus for peace—gives *Mexico City Blues* an aggressively hopeful tone.

Only in retrospect, in the last section of *Desolation Angels*, did Kerouac himself come to understand fully that the great faith he placed in Mexico derived from his own personal vision. In the process of an ill-fated move to California to be near his newfound Buddhist friends, including the poet Philip Whalen, Duluoz stops at the Mexican border with his mother, and together they walk over into Juarez. After lighting a votive candle for her dead husband in the church of Maria de Guadalupe and observing the penitents in devotion there, Duluoz's mother exclaims: "These are people who have heart!" (*Desolation Angels* 344). They are, in short, the "Mexico Fellaheen" Kerouac celebrated in *Lonesome Traveler*, kinsmen under the skin to the poor French Canadians from which the Kerouacs were descended, and fellow Catholics to boot. While Catholicism may have gained the upper hand in Kerouac's ideology during the later years of his life, it is clear that his memory of Mexico here is the memory of a time during which, thanks in large part to Buddhist doctrine, he had managed to suspend for a while the many conflicts of his consciousness. The narrator concludes this episode of *Desolation Angels* on a note of satisfaction with his mother's intuition about the place: "Now she understood Mexico and why I had to come there so often" (344). Kerouac's feeling for Mexico, which he erected many guideposts for in his novels, was a feeling for the people, their religion, their way of life, their earth. In 1955, he made a monument to the feeling, and as the art that manipulates and finally masters the divisions of his consciousness demonstrates, *Mexico City Blues* deserves a permanent place among our other literary monuments to that ancient land.

The function of Mexican words, settings, and myths in *Mexico City Blues*, though much simpler than the function of the autobiographical theme, is far less obvious. At first I conceived of it merely as a binding agent, a rather convenient, superficial element that serves to connect various aspects of the poem—some of them highly abstract—to a concrete sense of place. This is particularly true with respect to the Buddhist theme. While Mexico—especially the Native American side of it—does serve to ground the poem, as it grounded *On the Road, Dr. Sax, Tristessa*, and *Desolation Angels*, it plays other roles as well. Chief among these are the sound effects the Spanish language provides, the opportunity life in an ancient society gives the singer to illustrate his views on reincarnation, and the images foreign landscape and folkways contribute to the surrealism of the poem.

Several Spanish words occur with special force in the opening choruses of *Mexico City Blues*. *Ojo* (eye), for instance, which appears first in the "3rd Chorus" and then not until much later in the "155th Chorus," performs a dual function by establishing a link between the light imagery that dominates the poem and the round sound of the *o*, which Kerouac considered the most characteristic sound of the language.

Another striking Spanish word that occurs in the early choruses is the word for *word, palabra*, found in the "5th Chorus." At first, this chorus seems to be an insider's notation. Its first stanza, which is full of the *o* sound, introduces Gregory Corso, a latecomer to the Beat inner circle and the model for the antagonist in *The Subterraneans*, whose Italian surname takes on a Spanish accent. Then Kerouac mentions himself by what may be either an allusion to a line in "Howl" ("Kind king light of mind" [10]) or a reference to the end of *Visions of Cody* ("Adios, King" [398]). At any rate, he manages to work in the name of the second member of the Beat circle.

Next, he reveals that "William Lee," the author of *Junkie*, is really William S. Burroughs. Apparently Kerouac is enforcing his own standards of openness on Burroughs's fiction. Then he makes a statement that presumably alludes to his stay in a psychiatric ward during his brief service in the Navy in World War II. At one of his interviews, Kerouac identified himself to the military psychiatrist as Samuel Johnson (Charters 329), so this may be Kerouac's nom de guerre. Here, however, Johnson is "Under the sea," meaning perhaps that the subterfuge has been abandoned, Kerouac has shaken off his madness, and he is writing now in his own natural voice, unconstrained by eighteenth century conventions of craft. (It is also an allusion to Dr. Johnson's near fatal voyage to Scotland.)

The next-to-last stanza dissolves from a reference to Cole

Porter into pidgin Spanish that has undertones of nursery rhyme:
The

<blockquote>

parter

Of Peppers
Is Numbro
Elabora.

</blockquote>

I translate this: "My Mexican mask is the song I will now de-
velop." Of course, the stanza has many other potential meanings.
The important thing here, however, is the dissolution of autobi-
ography into demotic Spanish (or possibly even Italian, in honor
of Corso). It is as though Kerouac, through his singer, is re-
versing the process by which he became a writer: he is retracing
the steps of his acquisition of language. Just as in his childhood,
he finds himself in a situation where he must learn words first as
pure sound. This is an invigorating, if exhausting, circumstance.
The clarity that has begun to emerge by virtue of the first minor
triumphs of the four Beat writers disintegrates in the confusion of
a strange culture. The last stanza, brief as it is, provides a give-
away: in English, "you know what I" would normally be followed
by "mean." Instead we get *palabra*. In the context of Buddhist
logic, this locution ensures that the reader does not mistake the
word—as Spengler would say, the sign for a sign (2:149)—for
meaning, or for that matter, the meaning for essence. "You know
what I word" invents a way of opting out of the necessity to make
meaning. The singer is simply making words. Kerouac imagines
he is leading the other three writers—who were all busy exploring
foreign cultures during this period—into a more spiritually honest
style.

This pidgin Spanish also signifies a melding of cultures, a
theme that becomes evident in the "9th Chorus." Here, the "hero-
ines of Cathedral / Fellaheen Mexico," a reference not so much to
the church as to the Cathedral Indians (see the description of
Tristessa [*Tristessa* 10-11]), who are "Commenting on the Great
Cities / of the World." Spengler used the term "fellaheen" only in
passing and in a very technical sense. The import given its mean-
ing is all Kerouac's. The fellaheen, according to Spengler, who

distinguished this group from the "primitives" who precede the establishment of a great culture, are the remnants of a great culture that has already fallen (2:105). The word comes from the Arabic designation for an Egyptian plowman. Kerouac always uses the word to lend a sense of the transitoriness of civilization and the persistence of fundamental values. French Canadian by ancestry, he clearly identified with the fellaheen, and part of the message of *Mexico City Blues*, as of *Tristessa*, is that the members of sophisticated societies should learn humility from the dignity, beauty, and simplicity of these survivors of a culture that has fallen—as ours inevitably will also fall.

The fellaheen "Indian songs" ("12th Chorus") actually remind the singer of "little French Canuckian / songs my mother sings." One of these tunes probably refers to Ti Jean Kerouac himself: "Johnny Picotee," or Johnny with "the Poxy back" ("88th Chorus"). As in the "5th Chorus," the language sounds begin to get jumbled as they must have in Kerouac's childhood, leading to more made-up words, in this case, "Negwayable." Exactly what it is that is "unweighable" remains obscure, but the Spanish words *para* (for) and *ya* (already) that follow give some clue. The "Aztec squeaks" that the singer detects are both the sounds of fellaheen babies and the new sounds he is learning to make in the poem. "For already" is his way of indicating that he has some kind of connection that is "unweighable" yet palpable to him because it is "for" what has "already" happened. This makes the last line of the chorus a conclusion that reaches into the themes of autobiography and Buddhism: "(ONLY THE MOTHERS ARE HAPPY)." Kerouac wished desperately to escape the cycle of rebirths. Life for him meant suffering, yet he held motherhood sacred. He resisted seeing the agent of rebirth as responsible for suffering. In fact, he picks up the image of the womb from the sutras (the Buddhist scriptures), where it represents the perfect emptiness of the Tathagata, the completely perfected Buddha. In the "12th Chorus" even the assertion of conclusion is enclosed—made absent in its presence—by parentheses. Sound, by its sensuous immediacy, will eventually replace the arbitrary conceptions represented by ideas and words, as is exemplified by the conclusion of the chorus.

Before I take up the singer's previous life as an Indian, let me reiterate that Kerouac—like his countryman Thoreau—did express the desire to return to the simple ways of the fellaheen. This desire is set forth in the "64th Chorus," where the singer intones: "I want to go live in the desert / With long wild hair." This thought is repeated in the "138th Chorus" after an assertion of the similarity between the Brooklyn night and the Aztec night, and the singer even renames himself "Jaqui Keracky." In the poem Kerouac's real-life desire to live the life Thoreau led at Walden stands also for his recollection of previous lives. By returning to life in a hut, he imagines he is bringing his existence full circle.

The singer makes the story of rebirth explicit in a series of choruses, beginning with one that is set off by the songs of the Indian children, the "13th Chorus." The story, which begins on a humorous note, proceeds in a straightforward manner. The scene is probably associated with a sacrifice to the ancient sun god Huehueteotl, who is mentioned in the "207th Chorus." As was typical of Aztec sacrificial rites, here the victim's heart is removed while it is still beating. Gifford and Lee report that during Kerouac's visit to Mexico City in 1952 "Burroughs was still involved in his studies of Aztec culture . . . especially interested in the psychological terror methods used by the priesthood to maintain control over the population" (163). Making himself into the Christlike victim, Kerouac transforms the terror into heroism by returning to life in subsequent rebirths.

The imagery calls up his birth in Lowell. The color russet combines the red that signifies birth (as in the "89th Chorus": "red gory afternoon") and the brown that signifies security of childhood at home. The births are being consciously conflated. The upshot is a kind of mythic resurrection out of the mouth of the sacred volcano, Popocatapetl. As in two later choruses (the "21st" and "22nd"), the fellaheen theme mingles with Buddhism to produce a commentary on rebirth. When "they," presumably the priests, arrest the singer for the size of his heart, he decides not to return for further rebirths. This is the bodhisattva state of "no recension," and the size of the singer's heart is probably a way of symbolizing compassion, the virtue that distinguishes the bodhisattva and compels him to forego nirvana. This chorus fore-shadows the "140th Chorus," in which the singer describes his last rebirth, repeating the warning: "Don't Come Back."

The story of the singer's Aztec rebirth is concluded on the far side of the Lowell Canto. The "119th Chorus" recalls the image of the human sacrifice. Not only does the brutal rite prove ineffective in preventing the return of the singer in a subsequent life, but now, by virtue of his experience of rebirth, he reproaches the priests for their erroneous form of worship. "You better / get on back to your kind / boat," he warns them. The boat is presumably the SS *Excalibur*, later rechristened the SS *Mainline*, the bodhisattva's boat, which is "reeling in merit like mad" ("229th Chorus"). It is possible, too, since the singer uses the second person pronoun in this chorus, that he is reminding himself not to get wrapped up in the cycle of rebirths again but to get back to his Mahayana boat. (Mahayana, "the Great Vehicle," is the Buddhist sect or tradition with which Kerouac most closely identified his own beliefs.)

Finally, in the "127th Chorus," the singer reveals the details of his previous life among the fellaheen. Aside from the food and the presence of more than one sister, this life sounds very much like Kerouac's childhood in Lowell. In the poem, however, it all happened "incalculable / be-aeons ago." It carries the sense of a golden age, "when white while joyous / was also / Center of lake of light." Again the singer suggests that the outcome of rebirths for the enlightened one is present even in the beginning. This squares with Buddhist doctrine, which holds that the bodhisattva, in his final stage of accomplishment, realizes that his salvation was implicit in his existence from the very beginning. Kerouac, I believe, is also implying an analogy between Spengler's view of culture and the life of the individual soul. The establishment of a culture transforms the primitive into a civilized being, and the demise of the culture transforms him once again into a fellaheen. For Kerouac, the transformations—and here he differs radically from Spengler—are superficial. The essence of enlightenment is circular, involving a return to the state of nondiscrimination that prevails before birth. The Tathagata is one who recognizes no distinction between potential and fulfillment.

At the same time, Kerouac perceives something silly in all his speculations, and the Mexican choruses and the Spanish language enable him to relieve his suspicion of his own pretentiousness with humor. This results in a great deal of word-play, but it also engenders an absurdist drama that is performed sporadically throughout *Mexico City Blues*. This interpolated playlet is made, as the singer chants in the "31st Chorus," by a

> Convulsive writer of Poems
> And dialog for Saints
> Stomping their feet
> On Pirandelloan stage.

The absurd or surreal element in *Mexico City Blues* arises directly from the singer's discovery in the "24th Chorus" that all statements about the ultimate nature of reality amount to nothing more than whistling in the dark. According to Charters, Neal Cassady once told Kerouac: "Lyric is supported on bubbles, and what is too foolish to be said is sung" (165). It is easy to miss the humor in Kerouac because of his excitement or his melancholy, so I want to draw out this absurdist plot a bit facetiously, and perhaps more than it warrants.

As near as I can tell, in this story "Kerouaco" ("24th Chorus") ascends "Pis Cacuaquaheuro / Monte Visto de Santo / De Gassa" ("32nd Chorus"), or freely translated, "the Then-Addled Mountain of the Clear Sight of the Gaseous Saint," a place "where rosy doves're seen flying." On the mountain he conceives a mission, and after brief initial resistance from the "old euphonious phoney of Arkansaw" ("45th Chorus"), he falls in love with the comely and exotic "Asphasiax the Nymph of India" ("50th Chorus"). In a dream-vision, or perhaps as an aftereffect of his ascent of the mountain, he recalls his origins in the Spain of George Bernard Shaw's *Man and Superman*:

> The time we crossed Madrid
> in a car
> and Kelly pointed out

> the dreary Spanish
> Ar chitecture. ("77th Chorus")

From a balcony, he and his dream companions can see the "Porte Corriere," perhaps an image of the Dharma Door of the sutras. Their dreams turn westward, where the countryside of "Spanish / Portugy" is "Blazed / By guitars / Like Spanish Cows" ("78th Chorus"). In the dim distance another mountain rises, "Monte de eleor / De manta," or the "Mountain Shaped Like the Poet's Father With a Blanket Over His Head." Meeting a nebulous representation of a great Spanish philosopher, "Ortega y gassa," Kerouaco and his companions hurl crude curses at the intellectual:

> Fawt
> > Ta caror
> > Ta fucka
> > Erv old
> > > Men.

With the aid of a magic potion, perhaps a combination of morphine and marijuana, Kerouaco finds himself in "old hazisch Mexico / of Hashisch, Shaslik / and Veal Parmesan" ("134th Chorus"). His mission is one of quest and conquest, it seems, though the "Russian Spy Buses" are "Tooting / 'Salud'." Trekking out on the plains "Beyond Pascual / And the Cactus Town" ("135th Chorus"), he meets "Matador pan," a bullfighting god disguised as a loaf of bread, and "Pazatza cuaro," a shaman of mixed Italian heritage who wears a duck mask and causes Kerouaco to garble his words. He then seeks refuge with "Aunt Semonila / The Amapola Champeen / Of Yon Yucatan" ("136th Chorus"), who sets him on the right course.

Kerouaco alters a favorite disguise of his own—dressing as a fat man ("104th Chorus")—by donning a woman's clothes ("147th Chorus"). After receiving directions and a warning ("148th Chorus") from his unseen communicators, he passes through the "Purple O Gate" ("155th Chorus"). He is forced to eat a "Huge Food monster . . . with FLAN & Syrup" ("159th Chorus"). Subsequently he has several sexual adventures (the

"175th and "186th" choruses), one of which takes place in the "I-Don't-Know / district of Hellavides' / Devil Dang" ("186th Chorus"), by all accounts a very dangerous place. Weakened by these sexual trials, "Garty" (Kerouaco in disguise) is mistaken for a bona fide drag queen by a Chinese homosexual ("214th Chorus").

Following this close encounter, Kerouaco assumes the macho mask of "Bojangles Banghard," a satyriastic hoofer. It is in this form that he must undergo his final trial, recounted in great detail in the "222nd" and "223rd" choruses. Bojangles imagines himself to be in a realistic movie that suddenly turns surreal. Amid "silent separative corpses" he acts out the "Story of No-Mad." He meets the archvillains "Ignorino the Indian General" and "Asserfelter Shnard Marade, / the Marauding Hightailer / of Southern Slopetawia," who are perhaps really projections of his darker selves. In a soundstorm of syllables he subdues them both, resuming for an instant his female form ("Gert" in the "223rd Chorus"). In the sky after the final battle he sees a vision of his own sign: "*Such Is.*" He knows he has conquered the demons and that he is now safe. In celebration, he sings "a little ditty," the "Nada moonshine number" ("224th Chorus").

What remains to be said of the Mexican theme in *Mexico City Blues* is perhaps its most important aspect, the one that influences the sound of the poem most profoundly: the way in which the *o* sound comes to represent the accent of Mexico as it takes shape in the mouth of the singer, and how the sound of that accent mingles with the sounds of other themes in the poem, first to present meanings and finally to move beyond them.

Like most poems, *Mexico City Blues* uses sound as well as sense to organize itself. Like all great poems, it also uses sound in particularly elegant and innovative ways to intensify the effects created by the signs. Like very few poems of any description, *Mexico City Blues*, because of its jazz poetics, brings sound into the foreground, with the result that meanings often dissolve into music. Spanish words, since they were even more strictly oral than English words for Kerouac, seem especially appropriate to the music making of the poem, and though the *o* sound is not the most important sound in the poem, I use it here to illustrate in a preliminary way exactly how the dynamic between sound and sign works in Kerouac's poetry.

The *o* sound, the typical ending of masculine nouns and the first person singular present tense of verbs in Spanish, stands for the Mexican element in the poem. Kerouac makes this clear by adding -*o* to English words when he wants them to rhyme with Spanish words. He also sets the *o* sound apart by identifying its letter shape with the finger-to-thumb mudra (a ritual hand gesture) seen in Buddhist icons ("176th Chorus"), the Buddha yoke of the parable ("229th Chorus"), a ring of baloney ("190th Chorus"), and the "space hole" imagery that occurs throughout the poem (for example, in the "191st Chorus"). The singer makes it clear that the sound of the letter has visual analogues in a number of different thematic sign systems. Indeed, his own rounded lips visually represent this powerful vowel even as he is in the very act of producing it.

The *o* sound springs up in a bilingual pun at the very outset of the poem. The singer is ruminating over the national debt (only $275 billion at the time) when he is suddenly shocked by the realization that the concept of a billion gives some insight into the bodhisattva's vow to work for the enlightenment of all sentient beings. His eureka takes the form of the Spanish *Ojo*—meaning "eye," possibly the "God's eye" ornament, or even "important," which also represents the English exclamation *O Ho!* This gives him his first glimpse of parinirvana, "The Purple Paradise." The sound of the *o* is taken up in the "5th Chorus," where it acquires an Italian accent. It opens wide in a paraphrase of the conclusion of the Diamond Sutra (Goddard 106) in the "6th Chorus," which revolves around the lines "and so no Solo Universal Self / exists."

The linkage of the "12th," "13th," and "14th" choruses is also effected primarily by the *o* sound. This linkage begins, appropriately, in the word "Mexico" in the first line of the "12th Chorus," continues in the introduction to a silly phrase in the next chorus ("O the ruttle tooty blooty / windowpoopies") and in Popocatapetl, the name of the volcano sacred to the Aztecs. What's more, the top of the volcano, an *o* image itself, is figured by the singer as a "Hungry mouth," which ties it to the theme of paternity discussed earlier. The sound comes to immediate fruition of meaning in this image and in the signal words "Teotihuacan," "Ocean," and "Sallow" in the "14th Chorus."

Again in the "24th Chorus," where the singer ironically introduces a Spanish version of the author's name—"Kerouaco"—the *o* that marks the endings of the names of all the artists, both real and supercilious, becomes hypostatized in the image of "A bubble pop, a foam snit," modelled on a passage in the Surangama Sutra (Goddard 179). The process is reversed in the "25th Chorus": the "radiant irradiation" issues from a "middleless center" much like the letter *o* itself and finds expression in the repetition of the *o* sound in the final stanza:

> Is my own, is your own,
> Is not Owned by Self-Owner
> but found by Self-Loser—
> Old Ancient Teaching.

The singer causes the *o* to move freely from sound to image, from image to sound, practicing to free the sound from the letter, the letter from the word, and the word from the meaning.

When *Mexico City Blues* gets into full swing around the "50th Chorus," the singer begins to elaborate on a connection made in the "13th" and "18th" choruses, the connection between the *o* sound and the *oo* sound. This latter sound is by far the most important sound in the poem, and the relation between the elemental vowels stands for some kind of spiritual transformation. The true Kerouac fan will be quick to vouch for Kerouac's comprehensive grasp of the technique of sound in language—not that he abstracted it from pure speech as I am doing here, but that he did pay close attention to such matters in the practice of his writing. The singer amusingly—and I think intentionally—emphasizes the connection between the two sounds in the "45th Chorus," when he intones: "Euphonism, a softening of sounds." The word "euphonism" contains both sounds, in the order of their importance. Perhaps that's why the distinction the singer makes between euphonism and euphemism is disputed by "the old euphonious / phoney," a kind of karmic tax collector who exacts

what Euphonic
doesnt-matter
Really pronunciation
price.

At any rate, the "50th" through "53rd" choruses display
more clearly the interrelation between the two sounds. To begin
the "50th Chorus," the singer compares himself to Osiris, then
makes an allusion to Rimbaud's dictum about the derangement of
the senses. He imagines, in order to practice Rimbaud's method, a
nymph named Asphasiax, who

Dances princely mincing
churly jargots
In the oral eloquent air
of tents'
Canopied majesty.

The canopy is the "O canopy" of the "157th Chorus." In the
"50th Chorus," it is Buddha, the prime carrier of the *oo* sound
throughout the poem, who brings the singer down to earth. The
final stanza is ominous and full of *oo*: "Maybe I'm an Agloon /
doomed to be spitted / on the igloo stone."

The "51st Chorus" picks up a big round hit of *o* from the
word "Opium" and from some Spanish/Italian names before it
moves into a complex word/rebus/sound exchange. "Eye" here re-
calls not only "I" but also *ojo* to the wary reader/listener. Translat-
ing to sound, then, the men have "one [*o*] on the loon," while
one *o* "is Tathagata's / Transcendental / orb of balloon." The *o*
here is thoroughly suppressed by the image of the eye and by the
oo sound, though it does sneak into the image disguised as the
Emersonian shape of the eye and as the signification of the word
that embodies the fuller sound, "balloon," the chief image of the
poem.

In the "62nd Chorus" the *o* sound recalls the collaborative
poem written by Ginsberg, Cassady, and Kerouac in the late
1940s, "Pull My Daisy." In the Lowell Canto, however, the

sound is almost entirely banished, except for the striking last line of the "92nd Chorus," "In the windows of their snow slope," the chopped phrase "poop hope" in the "93rd Chorus," and a strong encore by "Gordo," the fat man, who manages to

>   explode
>   loud huge grunt-o
>   and disgust
>   every one
>   in the familio

in the "104th Chorus." This chorus ends on a defiant *o*: "Paste that in yr. Broadway Show."

The image of the bubble reappears in the next chorus, where its hollowness gives way to repeated *o* sounds: "Man is nowhere till he knows." The repetitions of "nowhere" continue into the following chorus, where the singer is reminded of his experience of enlightenment: "When I fell thru the eye of the needle / And became a tumbling torso / In the Univers-O." *Ojo* is also used to mean "eye of a needle" in Spanish. The sound of the foreign word was perhaps implicit in Kerouac's English phrase, so it naturally elicited the rhyming word "torso" and the addition of the mock-Spanish masculine ending to "universe."

With the sounds of the "Aztec Radio" playing in the background ("116th Chorus"), the children's cries of "Mo perro" in the streets are balanced by "Russian Spy Buses / Tooting / 'Salud'" ("134th Chorus"). Thinking of this balance and how it might resolve into meaning, consider a series of sounds from the next chorus:

>   Poop
>   Indio
>   Yo yo catlepol
>   Moon Yowl
>   Indian
>   Town & City.

I think this is supposed to be an imitation of drunken speech, but it is intriguing how the passage retrieves "poop hope" from a previous chorus, as well as the name of Popocatapetl, which it rearranges in a humorous and perfectly predictable way so that "yo yo"—that is, "I I"—is now popping out of the volcano's hungry mouth. Moon is associated with Buddha both by sound and by previous imagery (see the "6th Chorus"). "Yowl" may also be an allusion to Ginsberg's "Howl." "Indian" is a translation of the Spanish word in the second line. *The Town and the City* is the Spenglerian title of Kerouac's first published novel, the only one published at the time this poem was written. So much meaning is present in the signs, yet what is most striking in these lines is the way the *oo* sounds surround the *o* sounds. Some dynamic of meaning has built up outside the signification of the words—in their sound—but, of course, that meaning remains strictly untranslatable. So Kerouac translates the Spanish word into English, then refers it to his version of Spengler's distinction between Culture (the Town) and Civilization (the City). I can only guess that this is an extremely veiled reference to Kerouac's reincarnation among the fellaheen, perhaps even suggesting that *Mexico City Blues* is an Indian reworking of the early novel.

In this same chorus, the singer characterizes his poetics as "Mix-technique," implying by the play on the word Mixtec, a merging of cultural identities, but also intimating, in my terms, that a mixture of sound and sign is his special technical device. By the time the word *ojo* occurs for the second and last time in the poem (in the "155th Chorus"), I am prepared for an interpretive leap of faith. This time, "O J O," all upper case, comes after the "Purple O Gate" rather than before the Purple Paradise. The eye has been reborn, but it is now the eye without I, the eye—or womb—of the Tathagata. If—and this is my speculation—one removes the J (for Jack) from "O J O," what is left is *oo*, the sound of womb and Buddha, both. These letters actually appear in the "172nd Chorus" as the beginning of a tune, "OO dee de ree, / — a song I could sing / in a low new voice." It may be too precious to assert, but nevertheless it is my intuition in the face of a difficult text that Kerouac intended and attempted to transform the images in *Mexico City Blues* into oral sounds that would still carry meaning, but carry it in the same vague and suggestive way that music carries it. He accomplished this end by means of the "Mix-technique." It may be that he thought of his ear for music as a fellaheen gift suppressed by the sign systems of English language and culture. Whatever the case, he plays an amusing and rewarding game in which the *o* sound is eventually subsumed by the *oo* sound, producing meanings that are at once metaphysical, cultural, and poetic, meanings that occur almost subliminally, as in pure music.

To conclude this chapter, here is a brief reading of the central poem in the Mexican theme, the "207th Chorus," which occurs just before the singer announces his intention to end the poem ("209th Chorus"). Here, he picks up the phrase "Aztec Blues" from the "139th Chorus" to serve as a theme. Then, immediately, he characterizes the theme as an "Imitation of Pound." Though Kerouac had just finished reading *The Cantos* before he wrote *Mexico City Blues*, in *The Dharma Bums*, which was written several years later, Ray Smith, the Kerouac character, makes some disparaging remarks about Pound (23). Why does he wish to imitate the Modernist master here? Perhaps he has the structure of his own poem in mind, since he has already made several references to "cantos" (including "waves of cantos and choruses" in the "44th Chorus"). He may also have in mind Pound's manipulation of mythology and history to suit the circumstances of a greatly altered world. I think, however, that Kerouac is responding most directly to Pound's advice in *ABC of Reading* that poetry stick close to music.

The "207th Chorus" is ostensibly a series of quotations from Aztec flood myth. "HUETEOTLE" (for Huehueteotl), however, was actually a fire god carried over from the Toltec pantheon. This god demanded sacrificial rites like those described in the "13th," "14th," and "119th" choruses. While his name does literally mean "the old god," he was not, as far as I can tell, associated with water. Kerouac is manipulating the mythology—like Pound—to suit his own purposes. He renders the name of the Feathered Serpent, Quetzalcoatl, phonically—"GLED-ZAL-

WAD-LE"—discusses its origin, and declares that he is the "Serpent as the Sign of Flood," probably an allusion to the great Lowell flood of 1936, an episode in the town's history that brought about Leo Kerouac's failure in business and earned a central place in one of his son's novels (see also the "183rd Chorus"). The thought of it leads him to exclaim nostalgically, "Ah / Sax." He is thinking of the conclusion of *Dr. Sax*, written in Mexico in 1952, but still unpublished at the time. In that novel about his childhood in Lowell, Kerouac had used the myth of the eagle killing the serpent, an image closely associated with Mexico's mythic origin and national identity. Here, however, he fixes on a myth that combines the bird and the snake: rescue from evil is one with evil itself. The conclusion of *Dr. Sax*, indeed, makes this identification a spiritual inevitability. The feathers of the plumed serpent embody Kerouac's reasons for being in Mexico City in 1955: "escape, / flight, exile."

The singer ends this important chorus with an enigmatic little verse: "Snakes that Fly / Nail Eternity / To bye/." I take this to mean that the combination of evil and escape from evil in a single creature is equivalent to the connection between death ("bye") and nirvana. Eternity is emptiness. The slash indicates, moreover, that what follows "bye" may be substituted for it. What follows is a fanciful translation of the name of an Aztec sun-god, Tonatiuh, an eagle who received slain warriors and women who died in childbirth into heaven. The singer gives the meaning of the word as "Of the Sunken Your Ear." Mysterious, were it not for the previous reference to Pound. Emptiness—salvation—in *Mexico City Blues* is achieved finally when the singer can both hear and sing silence. The ear here is "sunken" because the singer recognizes he is already dead, inundated by the flood, like Dr. Johnson "Under the sea." It seems feasible that "TI UH" might be construed as "Your Ear," but "TONA" cannot mean "sunken." It can only mean "tone" or "sound," the same sound as in the final chorus:

> the first sound
> that you could sing
> . . . .
> with nothing on yr mind—.

By virtue of his experience in Mexico, Kerouac has learned to as-
cribe a new goal to his singer: to chant a poem in which mean-
ing—created by sound—comes more and more to resemble music,
but a poem in which, at last, pure sound carries us into the infin-
itude of silence.

5

From Signing the Blues to Singing the Blues

Music alone . . . can take us right out of this world, break up the steely tyranny of light, and let us fondly imagine that we are on the verge of reaching the soul's final secret.

On his first night out with Mardou, Leo Percepied, the Kerouac character in *The Subterraneans*, goes to a jazz bar called The Red Spot to hear Charlie Parker play. He notices, at some point, that Bird is "digging" Mardou and also looking into his own eyes

> to search if really I was that great writer I thought myself to be as if he knew my thoughts and ambitions or remembered me from other night clubs and other coasts, other Chicagos—not a challenging look but the king and founder of the bop generation at least the sound of it digging his audiences digging his eyes, the secret eyes him-watching, as he just pursed his lips and let great lungs and immortal fingers work. (19)

Already in mid-career—though slightly published—Kerouac imagines that an "immortal" Bird can sanction his artistic aspirations.

78

The moment, one of many devotional moments in his lifelong admiration for jazz and jazz musicians, epitomizes the relation between words and music in Kerouac's poetics, a relation that he made supreme use of in *Mexico City Blues*.

The beginning of Kerouac's solo in the world, his year at Horace Mann Prep School in 1939–40, coincided with the advent of a revolutionary new jazz style called bebop. Thanks to the presence of three important jazz enthusiasts among his classmates— Jerry Newman, George Avakian, and Seymour Wyse—Kerouac, whose taste proved to be impeccable, was immediately turned on to the most authentic version of the new trend. Wyse, a British boy already expert in the jazz tradition, became Kerouac's Virgil on a series of visits to Harlem to hear the inventors of bop. The city ended up sounding like paradise, and Kerouac's encounter with the new musical form revolutionized his life. It gave him a model by which he could contemplate, conceptualize, and finally invent a new poetics—a poetics that took shape first in his fiction in 1951 and later in his poetry. By the time he sat down to write *Mexico City Blues*, fifteen years after his introduction to bop, he was so comfortable with the analogy between his own improvisational method and the playing of the great jazz masters that it seemed unavoidable: " 'Bop' / Even on a sailboat / I end up writin bop" ("42nd Chorus").

As early as 1959, Warren Tallman, in an essay called "Kerouac's Sound"—the single most insightful piece of Kerouac criticism ever written—identified some of the reasons for Kerouac's attraction to bop and described the effects his spontaneous poetics had on his first four novels. Even without the benefit of historical perspective, Tallman made a number of acute observations, not the least of which is that Kerouac had a "feminine sensibility" (227). Chief among these is his connection of writing and music by way of the shared bohemian lifestyle of the Beats and the jazzmen. From the distance of thirty or forty years this may seem obvious, but I doubt that, at the time, many white Americans knew enough about blacks to be able to distinguish among a variety of lifestyles still available for them in an oppressive society. Certainly not many whites—or blacks, for that matter—appreciated the wild innovations of bop or cared how the crazy men who made the sounds lived. My point is that Kerouac's use of jazz in his composition, especially in his composition of *Mexico City Blues*, results from an attitude toward the world he shared to some degree with the great African American bop musicians.

Kerouac makes his attraction to the down-and-out immediately apparent to his readers, and that attraction is one of the important meanings—along with the sense of keeping musical time—of the term *Beat*. Being down-and-out himself put Kerouac in touch with many of the same feelings that give rise to the blues, the dynamo that powers all jazz, including bop. Being down-and-out did not, of course, make him black, any more than participating in Bill Garver's daily routine made him a morphine addict, but it did put him in a position analogous to that of the bop musician, a position in the world that allowed him to empathize with the frustration, anguish, and indomitability that brought the great blues voices into being. "Blues truth," as Dennis McNally explains, "seized Kerouac, ripped him out of the white world, made him companion to Ishmael and Huck Finn, thrust him into the twilight land between the races" (39).

The mere fact that Kerouac was white prevented him from achieving more. Because he learned to appreciate those aspects of African-American culture that gave rise to the blues, he could, like many white vocalists, approximate the blues as a musical style in his writing, but he could not himself write—or sing—the blues. He was bound by his heritage to allegorize it.

Other factors, however, made his approximation extremely authentic. Like many white jazz musicians, Kerouac rejected, at least for a while, his own middle-class values in favor of the sensuous sounds and rebellious meanings of jazz. The blues temporarily provided a way out of the stultifying post-war suburban white culture. Kerouac also found within himself a reservoir of sentiment that must have seemed like the equivalent of the blues: good old Celtic nostalgia. The melancholoy tone of most of Kerouac's books is as obvious as their down-and-out settings. His mythic view of his family resembles that taken by progressive African Americans: a period of incredible pain in the not-too-distant past had been preceded by a time of freedom, rich culture, and relatively exalted status. With a Wordsworthian eye Kerouac applied this mythical understanding not only to family history, which he took to be a descent from Breton nobility, but also to his personal life: his own childhood and his brother Gerard's few years on earth before him. So Kerouac's emotional attitude toward life, like his preference for skid row hotels and cheap, sweet wine in the 1950s, enabled him to simulate the blues with great sincerity. I do not mean to imply that *Mexico City Blues* is in any way disingenuous. Quite the contrary. Still, it is a poem by a white man, so its use of the blues, in method or in content, must be taken metaphorically.

In *The Autobiography of LeRoi Jones*, Amiri Baraka classifies Kerouac's writing alongside Allen Ginsberg's as apocalyptic religious poetry. Baraka calls it a "hyped up version of Joyce with a nod in the direction of black improvisational music" (158). The connection of Joyce and jazz is telling. It was Ginsberg, after all, who declared Kerouac to be the inventor of "spontaneous bop prosody," but from the perspective of an African American—and one intimately familiar with the music and the milieu of the 1950s—Kerouac's writing looks more white than blue.

To be sure, Kerouac had other models besides bop to suggest an analogy between writing and jazz. As Kenneth Rexroth pointed out in an article in *Esquire*, jazz-poetry readings have been happening in this country since the 1920s (qtd. in McDarrah 60). The association of poetry with music, which itself is as old as literature, was reinforced by the influence of modern French poetry, a tradition of which Kerouac is only one of myriad inheritors. Kerouac had been introduced to Rexroth—who had himself been an early jazz critic and participant in jazz-poetry collaborations—in San Francisco during the early 1950s, when cool jazz was already taking shape as a successor to bop. Kerouac was fully aware, then, that he was working within a well-defined white literary tradition. The testimony to his musicality, which I do not doubt for a moment, comes mostly from white musicians like David Amram, while for Baraka, Kerouac's writing remains a mere "nod" in the direction of African-American music.

Baraka, whose critique seems appropriate here because as a writer he was long associated with the Beats, also produced the first sociological study of jazz, the extremely readable *Blues People*.

Like Kerouac, Baraka viewed Charlie Parker as the consummate bop musician, and near the end of the book he even refers to *Mexico City Blues*. Although Baraka did not move to Greenwich Village until 1957, which means that his ideas could not have influenced the composition of Kerouac's poem, *Blues People* suggests other plausible reasons for Kerouac's metaphoric use of the blues as a method, structure, content, and name for his poetry.

In his discussion of the origin of the blues, Baraka observes that black music sprang from opposing forces: the individual isolation imposed by the working conditions of slavery and the religious gatherings that were the only social events permitted the slaves. Added to this contrast was the further distinction between the regularity of European melody and the variety of African rhythms. Not only was blues always essentially an improvised music, but it was also primarily a vocal music, according to Baraka (*Blues People* 28). Later in the development of the blues, many of the greatest singers would be women, a situation that suggests the sexual equality created when slavery forced men and women to work together in the fields.

As for the function of blues in African-American society, Baraka emphasizes that the music was more a vehicle of expression than an artifact. "Blues," he asserts, "is primarily a verse form and secondarily a way of making music" (*Blues People* 50). This priority may explain Kerouac's intuitive attraction to the blues as a medium for poetry. Among the other diverse functions Baraka discusses is the ability of blues to meld highbrow, middlebrow, and lowbrow tastes. Only after the growth of a substantial African-American middle class and the advent of bop did the blues in the form of jazz become a divisive force in the African-American community. Even then it continued to provide a different kind of common cultural ground between African-American and white musicians and bohemians. This power to join different classes and cultures is a power Kerouac surely wished to exercise both in his personal life and in his artistic career, so it was natural for him to try to fuse it with his new poetics.

In its heyday in the 1920s, the blues also became a performance music rather than a community affair. Blues singers and jazz musicians went commercial. A confessional music by content, blues lyrics made performers seem heroic in their struggle for self expression. Baraka concludes: "The Negro had created a music that offered such a profound reflection of America that it could attract white Americans to want to play it or listen to it for exactly that reason" (*Blues People* 149). Some white musicians opted to give up middle-class ways of life in order to play the blues, and Baraka gives an even more specific account of what may have attracted Kerouac to African-American music: "The role of the improvising—and usually non-reading—musician became almost heroic" (*Blues People* 152). The lack of a system of written notation perpetuated the natural method of improvisation, and Kerouac recognized undeniable ties between the origins of jazz and his own affinity for orality in language. In recognizing this analogy, he found that his own art took on a heroic cast.

This valorization of musicians grew primarily from the cultural isolation experienced by African Americans in general and later by black bop musicians in particular. Their isolation corresponds to the willful separation and alienation the Beats called nonconformity (following the tradition of Thoreau). "Parker, Monk, and the others," Baraka says, "seemed to welcome the musical isolation that historical social isolation certainly should have predicated" (*Blues People* 191–92). The boppers, it seems, transcended their condition by making it a quality of their music. Ironically, the pride these musicians took in their isolation created a public perception that bop was separated not so much by culture, but because it was "deep" or serious art—a perception that caused a precipitous decline in the popularity of jazz.

This pretention to high art undoubtedly appealed to Kerouac and led him to model his writing on bop, but the personality of Charlie Parker, the "inventor" of the style, provided a more immediate practical impetus. Parker even lived in the Village for a time (*Blues People* 232) mixing with the other black and white bohemians, artists, and intellectuals. Baraka's analysis of Parker's contributions to jazz is also significant in terms of Kerouac's admiration for the musician: "After the legitimatizing influences of commercial swing," Baraka observes, "Parker restored the human voice to jazz" (*Blues People* 227). Kerouac was struck by the perfect fit of the analogy between Bird's art and his own: like Parker, he sought to restore the timbre of the human voice to poetry after the legitimating influences of the New Criticism. He wished once again to be able to sing the sign.

Kerouac's two aesthetic manifestos, published several years after *Mexico City Blues* (and included in Baraka's influential 1963 anthology, *The Moderns*), both contain the injunction to "blow as deep as you want" (343). One, "The Essentials of Spontaneous Prose," also contains three other references to jazz. Under "PRO-CEDURE" Kerouac says: "Sketching language is undisturbed flow from the mind of personal secret idea-words, *blowing* (as per jazz musician) on subject of image" (343). In the very next sentence, under "METHOD," he recommends the use of dashes to replace other marks of punctuation and to imitate "rhetorical breathing (as jazz musician drawing breath between outblown phrases)." Later, following the heading of "CENTER OF IN-TEREST," he writes: "Tap from yourself the song of yourself, blow!—now!" (344).

The analogy between writing and playing or singing music seems obvious, but the details remain unclear. Sometimes Kerouac envisioned himself as a horn player, sometimes as a drummer, but the music he had in mind, whatever the instrument, always sounded with the timbre of the human voice. If Charlie Parker's thrust was to give his horn a voice, Kerouac's was to restore the vocal qualities of words. I want to maintain the distinction between analogy and identity carefully because in *Mexico City Blues*, though the epigraph uses the term "blowing," Kerouac cautiously separates his role from that of Charlie Parker. He identifies his voice in the poem as a singer—perhaps even a female singer—in the "188th Chorus." Just as the similarity between horn and voice led Kerouac to conceive the analogy between bop style and writing, the difference between the two allows him to distinguish himself as a poet.

Kerouac developed his taste for jazz early in his adult life, and it is now clear that in addition to the immediate satisfaction he got from the music he was also working out the principles of his poetics. "When Miles Davis played," Ann Charters noted, "Kerouac heard his trumpet sounding long sentences like Marcel Proust" (226). As this new sound worked on his sensibility, he began to realize that the only possible escape from the limits of realism lay in the direction of some analogy with music. He began to reject the very notion of craft and to believe that "the only way out of such self-conscious art . . . lay along the lines of musical composition" (Nicosia 336). Nicosia has also noted that "Kerouac's conception of poetry was also affected by the content of traditional blues" (217). The blues, this biographer maintains, "served as the perfect vehicle to express—as the bop musician did in pure sound—his immediate, ongoing response to the world" (218). The poetics that resulted from Kerouac's affinity for jazz recreates his actual experience of music. He strove to make signs sound again, and the result for the reader/listener is a poetry that is ideally as sensuously immediate as music. Its meaning trails after the pleasure of hearing.

Paul Garon's *Blues and the Poetic Spirit*, which connects classic blues, Freudian psychology, and surrealism, gives a good sense of the value of Kerouac's truly radical endeavor. Garon suggests that swing launched a white counterrevolution against traditional jazz, "but bebop represented a 'negation of the negation' and consequently a new affirmation, a vehement *rallying to principles*: indeed, its impassioned return to the roots is inseparable from its advance" (13). In espousing bop as the basis for his poetics, Kerouac asserted the deepness of his own roots in tradition. He set himself squarely against a trend away from the musicality of language—the trend following from the degeneration of Eliot's critical dogmas, hypostatized in New Criticism—which allowed for the supersession of sight over sound, sign over song. Garon quotes from André Breton's 1944 essay, "Silence Is Golden," in which the surrealist poet asserts that the duty of poetry is essentially to unify and reunify sound and sight. This is a mission Kerouac heartily undertook. The negative or rebellious aspects of *Mexico City Blues* may even be seen as a religious mission since the negation of silence that has negated sound provides an apt metaphor for the Buddhist project of the poem—that is, the elimination of arbitrary conceptions that becloud the true nature of reality: emptiness.

Garon articulates some striking insights into the sexual nature of the blues as well, insights that are certainly pertinent to

Kerouac's state of mind in the summer of 1955. "The dynamic in-terrelationship of projected gratification and actual frustration," he says, "is the key to the essence of the blues" (67). This statement is also significant in religious terms since *Mexico City Blues* ex-presses Kerouac's passionate desire to escape the suffering of the world. Remember, too, that at this time Kerouac was practicing celibacy as part of his Buddhist resolve to eliminate desire as the cause of suffering. The content of the blues was a perfectly appro-priate content for his poetry. In fact, this aspect of the music coin-cides with a major dilemma of Kerouac's life: the conflict between freedom from responsibility and desire for sexual satisfaction. In this limited sense, Kerouac's whole life was a blues, a dialectic of frustration and gratification.

The essential quality of the blues, however, has to do with style, with the method of presentation. Garon describes it in this way: "Thus, a blues song can be distinguished from a non-blues by the way in which the almost indefinable *manner* of the perfor-mance relates to primary process functioning; the words become secondary elaboration" (35). By primary process, Garon means the Freudian unconscious. That is—and I believe this holds true for much of Kerouac's writing, including *Mexico City Blues*—the style of the blues, presumably both the composition and the perfor-mance, puts both singer and audience in touch with the most ele-mental workings of the mind. This contact with the unconscious accounts, I suspect, for the sense that Gifford and Lee, among others, report with respect to *Mexico City Blues*: "Some of the choruses read like scat singing played back at low speed, words 'blown' for their musical values or their punning link to the sub-ject matter that Kerouac had in mind" (190). The form of the blues, which Baraka calls primarily a verse form, provided Kerouac with an analog to his intuition about poetics. He recalled to us that words are fundamentally sounds, and he committed himself to exploring their deepest significance by returning signs to song.

By a fateful coincidence, Charlie Parker died on Jack Kerou-ac's thirty-third birthday, 12 March 1955. Bird himself was only a year and a half older than Kerouac, and his death must have set the seal on Kerouac's already acute sense of mortality. Though mention of the recently deceased musician is severely limited to the "239th," "240th," and "241st" choruses, *Mexico City Blues* is clearly an elegy for Parker, and the inspiration of his saxophone work suffuses the poem. It was Charlie Parker who drew Kerouac and many others fully into the jazz scene. As Baraka says: "Bird was probably the patron saint of the generation preceding mine" (*Autobiography* 129). His choice of terms is appropriate to Kerouac's religious attitude as well, for if *Mexico City Blues* is an elegy, it is also a proclamation of Bird's sainthood, in both a Catholic and a Buddhist sense. These two purposes are, however, somewhat at odds. To canonize, the poet needs to imagine difference; to elegize, he needs to imagine similarity. Because of the demands made on Kerouac by this simple contradiction, the figure of Charlie Parker is probably the clearest and most accessible aspect of the blues theme in the poem. Because of its obvious human and artistic value, it would also be tempting to overestimate Parker's role as a figure in the poem.

The three Charlie Parker choruses actually come after the drama of *Mexico City Blues* has been completed, almost as though Kerouac had enacted this drama to justify his elegy. In retrospect, however, Parker's life also justifies the drama, especially in its religious dimension. As the "Perfect Musician" in the "239th Chorus," he takes on all the characteristics of a bodhisattva. He even resembles the Buddha physically. Contrast this with the manner of his death, which is strangely prophetic of Kerouac's own death fourteen years later: "Laughing at a juggler on the TV / after weeks of strain and sickness." Could any death be more anticlimactic, more mundane, more American? By presenting Parker as a paradox, Kerouac makes an effort to demystify saintliness and sanctify ordinary human behavior.

The "239th Chorus" also connects Bird with Kerouac's life in several ways. First, Parker's facial expression, which conveyed the message that "All is Well," rephrases Gerard's vision that "everything will be alright" ("19th Chorus"; see also *Visions of Gerard* 14, 65). Bird joins Gerard as one of the Christ-figures in Kerouac's typology. And he is directly connected to the poem's epigraph. The feeling of listening to Parker play was like "the perfect

cry / Of some wild gang at a jam session." That same feeling also
resembles "a hermit's joy"—that is, the joy of Kerouac's hermitage
in Mexico City as he wrote the poem. Further, Bird died a kind of
martyrdom "to reach the speed / Of what the speedsters wanted."
His figure is intimately related to the most important motives in
Kerouac's life and to one of the arguments of *Mexico City Blues*:
that the true artist is necessarily a bodhisattva as well. The great-
ness of Parker's art is that its forms merge with human behavior
almost off-handedly: "In mores and what have you."

Part of Bird's artistic stature lay in his limited recognition, a
great solace to Kerouac at this stage of his career and in his at-
tempt to affiliate himself with the fellaheen. These ideas are joined
to begin the "240th Chorus," which spiritualizes Parker's relation-
ship with his audience as in *The Subterraneans* episode. Here he is
"whistling them on to the brink of eternity." His instrument is lik-
ened to St. Patrick's staff, used to drive the snakes from Ireland,
probably both for its religious significance and because Parker
died just a few days before St. Patrick's Day. The conclusion of
this chorus is a grim one:

> we plop in the waters of
> >   slaughter
> And white meat, and die
> One after one, in time.

The brutal matter-of-factness of this statement and the crudeness
of its imagery represent the singer's last confrontation with the re-
ality of death. The tragic story of all life is the tale told by Charlie
Parker's art.

"And how sweet a story it is," the "241st Chorus" begins,
an abrupt reversal in tone. Then, directly after a description of
Bird's joy in music, the singer shifts tone again, this time to disin-
terestedness: "Anyhow, made no difference." The stanza that fol-
lows this statement concludes the sequence. It is a prayer asking
forgiveness that begins by referring to the passage from *The Sub-
terraneans* used to introduce this chapter, then expands on the no-
tion that Parker has, indeed, become the Buddha:

No longer Charley Parker
But the secret unsayable name
That carries with it merit
Not to be measured.

The gathering of merit that has been one of the missions of the poem is expressed in a transposition in the very first chorus: "Mersion of Missy" equals "mission of mercy." The bodhisattva defers his own salvation for the sake of enlightening others; Bird as Buddha is now in a position to dispense merit as an act of mercy towards other sentient beings including the singer. His role as Buddha here comes very close to the intercession of a Catholic saint as well. In any case, the singer's last request is that he "lay the bane" of death off him "and every body" ("241st Chorus").

I think it is a mistake to read the final chorus of *Mexico City Blues* as spoken in the voice of Charlie Parker, as Nicosia does (489). The voice is clearly that of the singer, who is commenting on his own act of singing by extending the theme of sound in relation to mind from the "118th" and "206th" choruses. By this point in the poem, the singer himself has become a bodhisattva, so when he chants "All's well!" to conclude the poem, he does it for the first time with his own authority. This point is better argued in the context of the blues, however, and I will return to several earlier choruses to show exactly how the singer's voice develops. Suffice it to say that Charlie Parker's role here is not unlimited. Kerouac has come to a realization of the art that binds them as well as the art that separates them. He makes it clear in the epigraph to *Mexico City Blues* that he wishes both to identify himself as a jazz musician and to distinguish himself as a poet. He accomplishes this feat by discovering a new voice for himself, a voice with its origins in the stylings of bop instrumentals, a voice that takes on profound religious significance in the course of the poem.

It takes quite a while for the singer to work up to the blues theme in the poem. The list in the "23rd Chorus" remains untapped until the singer's epiphany in the "75th Chorus" that "cantos oughta sing." Then the autobiographical choruses intervene before he can explore this notion. Finally, in the "116th Chorus"

he hears the music of an "Aztec Radio," which by its fellaheen vi-
brations causes him to assert that he is the "Great Jazz Singer."
Immediately he is struck by the ramifications of this assertion,
which he discusses in the "118th Chorus."

He pauses—as do the musicians in several other choruses—
while the meaning of his discovery sinks in. Sarah Vag (Vaughan)
songs are playing on the radio when he grasps, then forgets, "that
it's my own fault" ("118th Chorus"). The "fault" is arbitrary con-
ception—in this case distinguishing between singing and not sing-
ing. Like the spoken or written word, song is spiritually valuable
because it points by its very existence to its identity with what it is
not. In a sense the singing is also a fault at this stage in the sing-
er's enlightenment because he is still distinguishing the act of sing-
ing from the act of not singing. Instead of feeling remorse, how-
ever, he focuses on what he has learned:

> I wouldnt
> be writing these poems
> if I didnt know
> That I grasp I sing.

The poem appears to indicate the singer's progress toward enlight-
enment, a pointing in the right direction. To close he enunciates
the lesson: "I've had times of no-singing, / they were the same /
Music is noise, Poetry dirt." What would have been a double blas-
phemy for the unenlightened Kerouac now becomes a redoubled
expression of faith.

In the "132nd Chorus" he expands this line of thought into
a definition:

> Innumeral infinite songs.
> Great suffering of the atomic
> in verse
> Which may or not be
> controlled
> By a consciousness
> Of which you & the
> ripples of the waves

are a part.
  That's Buddhism.
  That's Universal Mind.

Although he himself has mouthed some of the songs, he now reflects that they express pure suffering: the essential quality of existence, according to both Buddhism and Kerouac. These songs, he believes, are really the poetic embodiment of suffering, and while they are nothing in themselves, they may yet serve to lead him to further enlightenment.

Next, leading up to his summation of song in the final chorus, the singer presents a brief for what Allen Ginsberg called "spontaneous bop prosody" (*Howl* 3). Here in the "195th Chorus," "the songs that erupt / Are gist of the poesy," the singer declares, because they reveal his fundamental humanity. The stars, too, make a music that is the paradigm for the enlightened singer: "real, / Unreal, singsong, spheres:—." Kerouac uses both his spontaneous poetics and the Ptolemaic music of the spheres as warrants to reject standard religious poetry. I base my interpretation on a disjunction between the two halves of the third stanza. At first it seems the singer might be equating spontaneous poems with "human poetries / With God as their design," but then he cuts loose:

  And rip me a blues,
  Son, blow me a bop,
  Let me hear 'bout heaven
  In Brass Fluglemop.

The very silliness of the last word, a mutation of *flugelhorn*, emphasizes that the spontaneity of jazz singing rather than the "design" of human poetries leads to the realization of Universal Mind.

The "206th Chorus" is the last stop before the poem's conclusion. In a manner reminiscent of the closing sections of "Song of Myself"—another long American poem built by analogy to music—Kerouac's singer compares his act to the call of animals that open their mouths "to say something empty." He cannot yet ac-

91

complish this singing of pure sound, but he has perceived the final stage in his striving. "Open yr mouth with poems / without you make sound" is the step immediately preceding perfectly mindless singing. This may seem odd since most readers learn that meaning is the object of poetry, but for Kerouac meaning is only a means. His object is to make sounds like Bird Parker's saxophone, redolent of the human voice but emptied of arbitrary conceptions of significance. He echoes the aphorism of the "118th Chorus," broadening it to read "sound is noise." He now recognizes, in terms of the sutras, the value of "all sentient / communication." Such communication—words, music, animal noises—is "pointing to the finger / that points at sound / saying 'Sound is Noise'." This recognition justifies the existence of communication as a means to enlightenment:

> Otherwise
> sound itself
> un-self-enlightenable
> would go on blatting
> & blaring unrecognized
> as emptiness and silence.

For Kerouac's singer, the word is the sound that leads to silence.

The finale of the singer's apology for his own singing comes in the first two stanzas of the "242nd Chorus." It is a conundrum that may incorporate an allusion to John Updike's story "A&P." In this chorus, sound, which is now located by the singer in the mind, "is the first sound / that you could sing." But the condition here is crucial: "If you were singing / at a cash register / with nothing on yr mind—." I speculate that the cash register is a reference to Updike's adolescent narrator, who imagines that the supermarket cash register plays tunes. There is no source in the poem for this image. Despite this discontinuity, the gist of the lines comes through. True mindlessness, in its positive Buddhist sense, is its own sound, the sound of silence, so to speak. Nicosia, in fact, relates these two stanzas to the Diamond Samadhi, "the experience of hearing the hush of soundlessness, which is supposed to illustrate the Buddhist truth that existence is mind-created" (489). By extrapolating from his knowledge of the blues, Kerouac brings himself to a musical realization of a religious truth, and the religious truth reinforces his reliance on the music as method, form, and content.

The last part of my discussion of the blues theme in *Mexico City Blues* is both the simplest and the most difficult; here I will show how Kerouac manipulates language sounds to accomplish poetic, musical, and religious ends. As I suggested in tracing the Mexico theme, one sound—in that case, the *o* sound—apparently became associated in Kerouac's mind with the Mexico theme. The same is true of the blues: in this case, it is the *oo* sound, the very vowel of *blues* itself and by far the most important sound in the poem. A close listener can chart a progression from the *o* sound to the *oo* sound, a progression that indicates spiritual as well as musical evolution.

The constellation of meanings elicited by the *oo* sound in *Mexico City Blues* is immense, and Kerouac's affinity for the sound probably dates from his earliest childhood. It is, for instance, one of the sounds of his surname, which, Nicosia reports, was often mispronounced (21). It seems natural—childlike—that Kerouac would want to play with the sounds of his own name. To be sure, he often uses the *ack* sound that made his nickname rhyme with his surname to make fun of himself in *Mexico City Blues*. (See, for example, the "13th," "119th," and "137th" choruses.) He perceived this as the rhythmic or percussive element in his name, while he saw the *oo* sound as embodying the melody. The *oo* sound is also the vowel sound of both Kerouac's and Gerard's infant nicknames. Kerouac was "Ti Pousse" (Little Thumb)—see the "10th Chorus"—while the family dubbed Gerard "Ti Loup" (Little Wolf).

Among a host of associations that become apparent to the biographically informed reader/listener of *Mexico City Blues*, the *oo* sound also operates in the name of one of Kerouac's favorite authors, Marcel Proust; in many of the Sanskrit and Chinese words associated with Buddhism, such as *sutra* and—of supreme importance—*Buddha*; and in the linguistic sign for the most important image of the poem, *balloon*. This sound is associated with the distinctive timbre of the saxophone as well, and it carries the style and message of bop almost single-handedly throughout the poem. In this role it wages a musical battle with a watered-down romantic style that denatures melodies by neglecting or adulterating their blues roots. The purpose of this sonic conflict is to make a flank attack on romantic love. I will try first to follow this specific use of the *oo* sound, then I will return to a more general discussion of the way the sound helps organize the poem on the principles of blues and bop.

Unlike the thematic aspect of blues in the poem, which does not really catch hold until after the "75th Chorus," the *oo* sound is the first vowel in *Mexico City Blues*, in the word "Butte." The assault on romantic style, however, is deferred until just before the Lowell Canto. A "foresounding" does occur in the "16th Chorus," though, where the singer has already begun to investigate the path to enlightenment. The traditionally resonant image of the moon, with all its connotations of reflected light, chastity, and madness— all of which also operate in the poem—is found here in a "Cave inward." This cave is anything but romantic in the American musical sense. Autobiographically, the moon image probably comes from Kerouac's rooftop dwelling on Orizaba Street in Mexico City. What it inspires in him, however, is a desire to find the true path, the "One Way." This path is grounded in reality and sensuality:

> In the June
> of black bugs
> in your bed
> of hair earth.

The rhyming words "moon" and "June" are the staple of the American romantic serenade, and Kerouac sets about deconstructing their meaning in the poem.

Not unexpectedly, then, he starts to work seriously on them late in the Suicide Prelude, in the "81st Chorus." His attack is provoked (ostensibly) by Garver's singing of the words: "You'll never know / just how much I love you" ("80th Chorus"). He makes a "pome" out of Garver's bacon and eggs by turning them into a surreal couple, "Mr Beggar & Mrs Davy." The mood, carried by the lyrics of the previous chorus, is saccharine: "Looney and CRUNEY." After repeating this phrase with a change in spelling to emphasize the *luna* in "Looney," he proceeds, in a rather crude imitation of African-American dialect, to convert the poem about bacon and eggs into a bop trumpet solo:

> Ya gotta be able
> to lay it down
> solid—
> All that luney
> & fruney.

In the following chorus, the singer really begins to jam on the melody, and he ends with a kind of furious parody: "Looney & Boony / Juner and Mooner / Moon, Spoon, and June." Already it is clear that the target is the 1890s classic "Harvest Moon." In typical blues fashion, Kerouac immediately draws out the repressed sexuality of the romantic lyrics: "The orgasm / Of the moon / And the June." When he breaks into the lyrics of "Harvest Moon, "his memory fails him. His last halting words are "Croon— / Love— / June—." He concludes by rejecting the very idea that the right words are important; presumably, it is the tune that counts. In the "85th Chorus" he defines his new form—a tune without words (not, however, an instrumental)—as

> An asinine form
> which will end
> all asininity
> from now on.

This chorus is addressed to "Mr." William Carlos Williams, the suggestion being, I suppose, that Williams's imagism relies too heavily on the visual properties of words. Kerouac's new song, on the contrary, is: "The poem / Will end / Asininity."

According to Nicosia, the song "Harvest Moon" may have had extremely bad connotations for Kerouac (104). While he was imprisoned at Newport Naval Station in December 1942 for refusing to perform his duties, he shared a cell in the mental ward with a young Frenchman who sang the song incessantly. It is conceivable that, in Kerouac's mind, romantic love and madness were melded in the song. Certainly, in the Buddhist context, love and madness represent two forms of illusion that both prove and distract from the proof of the fundamental illusion of reality. That the conjunction of these two themes is highly significant is confirmed by the beginning of the Lowell Canto, where the singer joins the story of Kerouac's second marriage with the story of "all the crazy people" he's known, himself among them. The first occurrence of the *oo* sound in the Lowell Canto comes in the "89th Chorus." The words brought together by the sound show severe emotional disturbance. In the first stanza we find the "immense morning I was conceived i the womb, / And the red gory afternoon delivered / therefrom." This chorus concludes: "Wild howl the Lupine Cold the Moony / and Loony nights." I surmise that by the summer of 1955 Kerouac had begun to associate his suspicions of his own madness with his failed marriages. Here, the blues—underscored by the unusually long lines—reveals in sound effects what the practice of Buddhism revealed spiritually: that concepts of love and sanity are both devices by which the ego preserves the manifest illusion of its own integrity. Though the *oo* sound itself continues to develop in the Lowell Canto, this particular aspect of it culminates in the "95th Chorus" in a specifically musical connection. The sound, suggested in the words "door" and "neighborhood," comes out roundly in the name of the street, "Beaulieu," the location of the house where Gerard died. Now the singer delivers a pointed remark that reflects on the "moon-June" romanticism: he describes "pests of tenement crooners, / Looners—." The implication here is clear: not only has Kerouac associated love and madness as dangerous forms of illusion, but he has also identified the crooner as the prime purveyor of these illusions. His whole career had set itself against becoming such a crooner, and here he uses his childhood memories to provide a stark contrast to the kind of singer he now wishes to be.

Although the *oo* sound figures in more than a third of the choruses of *Mexico City Blues*, in order to investigate its more general function in the poem, I will focus only on several instances in which its presence is overwhelming. In this last part of the chapter, I will be show how Kerouac employed the essence of the blues as an organizational principle in his long poem.

The *oo* sound actually begins the "1st Chorus" on the downbeat of the bass drum. After meaningful but isolated occurrences of the sound in the next few choruses, the singer takes it up playfully in the "13th Chorus." Just after a gruesome image of human sacrifice, he improvises this riff:

> O the ruttle tooty blooty
> windowpoopies
> > of Fellah Ack Ack
> > Town.

These lines are rich with references to Kerouac's birth, the river in his hometown (for a similar allusion see the "210th Chorus"), and even his name. Since this entire chorus is devoted to the theme of reincarnation, the meanings suggested by the sounds form a kind of substratum for the meanings carried by the words. As the linguistic meanings take shape, they are continually reinforced or undercut by the "soundtrack" of the poem.

After many more significant occurrences—including the connection of the blue sky with the repetition of the word "balloon" in the all-important "27th Chorus"—the *oo* sound erupts again in the "37th Chorus." This chorus contains one of only ten or so specific references to jazz musicians, in this case, the saxophonist Lester Young—Neal Cassady's musical hero—"in eternity / blowing his horn alone." His tune will "smooth out the rough night." In the middle of this chorus the singer heaves a sigh that is almost inexplicably deep. "Ah Patooty," he exclaims,

> Teaward Time
> Of Proust & bearded
> > Majesty
> In rooms of dun ago.

Another form of "Patooty" appears in one of the Charlie Parker choruses, where the singer refers to Bird's axe as a "patootle stick." A similar word also occurs in the "209th Chorus"—"partotooty"—and in the "217th Chorus"—"prapopooty." I think these coinages come from an exclamation (Patoot!) or an old-fashioned term of endearment for a child (patooty), as well as from the Latin root *parturire*, "to be in labor." Intuitively, I suspect they all refer to birth. Other words in the "37th Chorus" support my interpretation. Proust, of course, is emblematic of memory in Modern literature, and the "rooms of dun ago" call up Kerouac's association between the color brown and his childhood homes. The sigh, I believe, originates in the deep association between the *oo* sound and birth in his mind.

The "63rd" and "65th" choruses make the first extensive connections between the *oo* sound and Buddhism. These effects are fairly straightforward, however, and I will note only how convenient the Hindu terms and place names are to allow the singer to bring the sound to bear without strain. It is impossible that a careful wordsmith like Kerouac would not have been *primarily* attracted to the sounds of the words in his newfound religion. He makes that attraction part of the form of *Mexico City Blues*.

The "72nd Chorus," on the other hand, presents problems. It is a good example of a chorus that makes little sense without reference to the organizational properties of the *oo* sound. I identify the "Book of Pluviums" ("73rd Chorus") as the text written for the absurd drama that takes place within the poem. As such, it might be regarded as a microcosm of the book it is part of—that is, *Mexico City Blues*. It is the "book of rain," a kind of watery blues itself. But its main characteristic is logical and semantic intractability. It is a little book organized solely on the basis of sound. The singer plays with sounds that double as letters and words—"A O Kay"—which are also constituents of Kerouac's name. He asks for advice just as he hears the bus go by on the street: "Zaroomoo." He acknowledges the central sound of the Book of Pluviums. Then he hears the "Nay Neigh / of the Heaven / Mule" and wonders if it will be possible to translate the Mule's neigh (or nay, for that matter) into sound as easily as he has translated the noise of the bus. This concern calls up several Sanskrit-sounding words; however, these words appear incomplete. The *mer* sound associated with the singer's mission in the

poem ("mercy" and "merit") occurs twice. "Yes / Sir," the absurd-
ist concludes, burping with merit and mercy, "HOOT GIBSON."
Hoot Gibson, of course, was a singing cowboy, one of many
who, against both realistic and dramatic odds, saved the day and
lived to sing again. He is one of the heroes admired by the author
of the "Book of Pluviums."

Sometimes, as in the "98th" and "109th" choruses, the *oo*
sound worms its way into rhyming words (in the style of the Gin-
sberg-Cassady-Kerouac poem "Pull My Daisy") in parodic protest
against the crooner's use of the same sound in his romantic bal-
lads. But one of the densest instances of the sound comes in the
fantastically rich "137th Chorus." Here, the first occurrence of the
sound comes in the word "BLUES," which is followed by a per-
cussive rearrangement of the sounds of Kerouac's last name. "Cit-
lapol" is probably a phonetic rendering of *citlatepetl*, the Aztec
word for Mt. Orizaba, the highest peak in Mexico, after which the
street where Kerouac lived in Mexico City was named. So the
"dobe roofs" include his own little rooftop hut in the city. Again,
as in the "72nd Chorus," ambient noise intrudes, this time in the
sound of scraping chair legs. The singer tries his hand at singing
the sounds made by various entities. The "Ferwutl" of the "Beard
Bird" is perhaps the most entertaining in its combination of the *oo*
sound with an Aztec form. The "Howl of the Moondogs of Mon-
terrey" sounds the close of the poem with a noise that comes from
a ring around the moon, the sound of the image in the shape of
an *o*.

The finale of the *oo* sound in *Mexico City Blues* is a part of
the "Fonally finalles" in the "223rd Chorus." Concluding the
poem means, for the singer, "Hookies from OO-SKOOL," a
phrase that also has autobiographical significance for Kerouac,
who supplemented his income for a while by signing up for
classes at the New School for Social Research in New York to get
his GI benefits. The singer sings with exuberance here, with a
sense of his successful performance. Even the Indian boy of his
fellaheen imagination is crying his favorite sound: "Wu!" The
singer cuts loose with a riot of sound that drowns out many of
the important images and meanings—iron, moon, wheel, lake,

honey—present in the chorus. He drives toward a significance that comes from sound, rather than a signficance that merely happens to have a sound:

> Sound
>> E Terpt T A pt T E rt W—
>> Song of I Snug Our Song
>>> Sang of Asia High Gang.

He finds that even his Buddhist theme will wind up as music rather than meaning, and that it is safer and surer that way.

The singer recalls, briefly, Kerouac's work on the Southern Pacific Railroad ("Ole Watson Ville" being a substation on the railroad) and decides that a good way for him to define memory is as "noise of old sad so," almost like Burns's "Auld Lang Syne." The words *"Such Is"* in italics signify the state of the void, of perfection, the Tathata. To sing with *oo* rounded lips marks the climax of a spiritual quest in musical terms, to make poetry without reliance on arbitrary conceptions. In this state of sonic abandon, practically egoless, the singer winds up with a ridiculously profound ditty: "Sing a little ditty of the moon inside the loony / boon of snow white blooms in Parkadystan / I S T A M H O W H U C K." The song is now inside the *oo* sound, which is all that is left to give it meaning. Like the image of the balloon, the *oo* sound epitomizes "man in the middle" (see the "2nd Chorus"), the human being who has destroyed all tendencies toward reliance upon arbitrary conceptions. The last line, I speculate, refers to Twain's hero having finished his trip downriver. It may even contain a question, something like: How is it that I am now Huck? It may be facetious, but the answer is that the singer's ferry/fishin' ship/raft has brought him down river, his inheritance is secure, and he will now be off for Indian territory.

If one were to judge the importance of the blues in *Mexico City Blues* based on content, it might easily be underestimated. There are only twenty or so direct references to jazz, against well over a hundred references to literary figures. Yet as a method of composition, a verse form, and a style of performance, bop provided the formative analogy for the poetics Kerouac has exercised so brilliantly in these 242 choruses. As a means of organizing a long poem, bop brought Kerouac as close to the bardic model as a Postmodern poet could hope to get. This means—the musical analogy—is not unique to Kerouac, but his execution, his performance, his mastery, it seems to me, are beautiful beyond words.

6

Kerouac's Religion(s)

Buddhism, which only a mere dabbler in religious research would compare with Christianity, is hardly reproducible in the words of the Western languages.

Near the end of *Desolation Angels*, Kerouac, describing his attempt to make a home for himself and his mother in the Berkeley Hills, attributes the following remark to her: "You and your Buddhists! Why don't you stick to your own religion?" (351). If it was an appropriate question for the mother to ask her son in the 1950s, it is an even more appropriate question for the literary critic to ask the text today. Why did a writer nurtured on French-Canadian Catholicism go to a profoundly Catholic country like Mexico to practice his understanding of Buddhism in the blues form of his poetry?

Biographer Tom Clark says that Kerouac began to study Buddhism in Asvaghosa's *Acts of the Buddha* while he was living in Richmond Hill in the winter of 1953–1954 (131), although he had certainly become acquainted with it much earlier through his reading of Thoreau and Spengler, and later, in the spring of 1953, through Allen Ginsberg's study of Oriental art. After the war, a

102

general interest in things Oriental pervaded American society, and books like Dwight Goddard's *Buddhist Bible*, reprinted in 1952, became more readily available. As a literary phenomenon, of course, Orientalism was nothing new in America, but in the 1950s it quickly reached the proportions of a subculture, one that still flourishes today. Kerouac was among those who rode the crest of a wave that swept over the materialism of that decade.

When Kerouac arrived at the Cassadys' home in California in February 1954, he discovered that Neal and Carolyn were doing two things that greatly annoyed him: first, they were planning to buy a new house with the proceeds of a personal injury suit Neal had filed against the railroad; and second, they had become followers of Edgar Cayce (Nicosia 457). Since Kerouac had already begun to read Buddhist texts, it is fair to assume that his interest satisfied some positive need for spiritual guidance, but it is equally fair to say that among his motives for continuing to read the Eastern scriptures was a newfound need for arguments with which to counter the Cassadys' Cayceism. The value of Buddhism as apologetics can be felt in *Mexico City Blues* as the severely diminished presence of Cassady—who was the model for Dean in *On the Road* and the inspiration for *Visions of Cody*—as either a character or an influence. At the very moment Allen Ginsberg was addressing their old friend Cassady as the "secret hero" of "Howl," Kerouac was at pains to obliterate him from *Mexico City Blues*.

One of the most poignant choruses in the poem, however, comes in the form of a letter possibly addressed to Cassady. The tone of the "114th Chorus" is both wistful and conciliatory, as though Kerouac sensed that his association with Cassady had come to an end and he wanted to part on good terms. The first stanza recounts a coincidence that the singer has detected in an exchange of letters: perhaps Kerouac and Cassady had discussed the same topic in letters that crossed in the mail. Next, the singer explains that all their troubles are past. At first, this seems to be a way of saying that his Buddhist studies will make him a better friend in the future, but the tone gives these lines an ominous implication as well. Kerouac senses that he will not be spending much time with his old friend in the future. Then he generalizes by alluding to one of Cassady's favorite musicians, Lester Young: "The sweetest angelic tenor of man." He identifies himself with the tenorman by placing him in the context of the epigraph, which is rephrased here in the third stanza. The chorus concludes with a compliment to Cassady and a metaphysical twist: "I've gone inside myself / And there to find you." My sense of this chorus is that Kerouac, who once made Neal his hero, has now assimilated him into his Buddhist practice, specifically his quest for anatta, release from selfhood.

On the other hand, in a more positive light, Buddhism seems to have served as the dynamo that powered Kerouac's poetic impulse. The first book he wrote after beginning his study of the sutras, *San Francisco Blues*, was composed in the Cameo Hotel during the spring of 1954 while Kerouac was working as a brakeman on the Southern Pacific. While it has neither the coherence nor the magnitude of *Mexico City Blues*, it does indicate the direction in which Kerouac's writing was impelled by his newfound religion. A certain stillness in these blues poems contrasts markedly with the motion of his novels. The observation of detail, which is great in both the fiction and the poetry, seems to be externalized, objectified, detached. The philosophical content, which is much more apparent in the poems than in the novels, flows directly from Kerouac's focus on the details of daily life on skid row. He gives a strong sense that the characters, their actions, and the world in which they occur are all illusory. In short, Buddhism provided Kerouac with a new mode of imagination, one that complemented and supplemented his fiction.

In his book on the history of Buddhism in America, Rick Fields summarizes Kerouac's investigation of Oriental scripture and describes his unpublished Buddhist writings: "*Some of the Dharma* (which had become an elaborate scrapbook of musings, *pensées*, sutra extracts, aphorisms, haikus), *Wake Up*, a biography of the Buddha, and *Buddha Tells Us*, a collection of translations" (211). Fields also expresses great esteem for *The Scripture of the Golden Eternity* (written in 1956 and published in 1960), calling it "one of the most successful attempts yet to catch the emptiness, nonattainment and egolessness in the net of American poetic language" (216). The unpublished works preceded *Mexico City Blues* in order of composition, while *The Scripture*, written under the influence of Gary Snyder, followed it within a year. Kerouac spent most of his writing time during 1955 working on these various Buddhist texts, and when he was not writing about Buddhism, he was usually reading, thinking, or talking about it. He was fortunate, as well, to find a community of fellow writers, including Snyder, Ginsberg, and Philip Whalen, who shared the intensity of his interest.

Robert Hipkiss, who has written about Kerouac's romanticism, asserts that Kerouac's "quest for the infinite led him to Buddhism as a means of cleansing perception" (64), following one of Blake's "Proverbs of Hell." Hipkiss rightly perceives that Kerouac's "primary allegiance was . . . to Mahayana Buddhism" (67), which he preferred to Zen "because he wished to de-emphasize the cycle of earthly existence and concentrate on union with a Godhead" (71). He summarizes Kerouac's Buddhism this way:

> Kerouac interprets the Buddhist attitude toward the illusions of our senses as follows: first, because they are factitious they are essentially meaningless; second, because they are meaningless there is no point in labelling them good or evil; third, because the world has no true reality and there is no good or evil, there is nothing for us to do in it except to exist, to accept the wonder of illusion, to be kind to all who are afflicted by it and to know that death marks the end of it and a return to the perfect void. (66)

Unlike most other commentators, Hipkiss concludes that Kerouac's investigation of Buddhism exacerbated the instability of his thinking. "By refusing to establish a balance between uncontrollable forces of life on the one hand and death on the other," Hipkiss believed, "he shifts from one absurd view to the other" (72).

Eric Mottram characterizes the standard interpretation in his introduction to the second edition of *The Scripture of the Golden Eternity*: "Throughout *Mexico City Blues* . . . the presence of what Kerouac had learned he needed from Buddhism enlivens and guides the poet's desire for active equilibrium" (xi). Nicosia finds this equilibrium also embodied in Kerouac's novella, *Tristessa*, the narrative "stretched taut between the antipodes of Buddhism and Catholicism, between the subjective depreciation of life and the objective desire for it" (477). Nicosia's opinion of *Mexico City Blues*, which Kerouac wrote at the same time as the first part of the novella, also implies balance: according to Nicosia, it "is a Buddhist book that talks itself back into a Christian love of life" (480). Despite that Kerouac's Christianity entailed a good deal of asceticism and that his resort to Buddhism stemmed from his desire to escape the emphasis on suffering he learned from his Catholic upbringing, Nicosia's analysis comes close to hitting the mark. Kerouac needed Buddhism; that is clear. But he also needed Catholicism. His was a deeply divided mind, and his theology reflects the division. Kerouac, I believe, *passed through* Buddhism in 1955 and 1956, and during these years the movement of his writing, like a satellite in orbit, achieved equilibrium.

Toward the end of the 1950s, Kerouac contributed an excerpt from *The Dharma Bums* to an issue of the *Chicago Review* devoted to Zen. In that same issue, Alan Watts, the great popularizer of Buddhism in this country, formulated a set of distinctions that is still helpful in trying to understand Kerouac's religion. Watts characterizes contemporary American Buddhism in social terms. He warns that there is "a kind of Western Zen which would employ this philosophy to justify a very self-defensive Bohemianism" (5). The question about Kerouac's Buddhism may be, as the title of Watts's essay ("Beat Zen, Square Zen, and Zen") suggests, whether it is beat or square, or neither. (Remember that Kerouac himself considered Zen too intellectual for his purposes, so we can simply think "Mahayana" when Watts writes "Zen.") Beat Zen, according to Watts, places Buddhism at the service of a very Western desire to rebel against the status quo. "Zen is fuss," he says, "when it is mixed with Bohemian affectations" (11).

"Foreign religions," Watts goes on to say, "can be immensely attractive and highly overrated by those who know little of their own, and especially by those who have not worked through and grown out of their own" (10). I feel a grave doubt, not about Kerouac's understanding of his own Catholicism, but about whether he ever "worked through" or "grew out" of it. Kerouac's Catholicism, independent and arbitrary as it was, re-

mains itself something of a mystery. He stopped attending mass in
early adolescence, yet his allegiance to the religion into which he
was born, like his allegiance to the lower middle class, was un-
swerving. Still, all believers entertain heresies about their faith,
and it may very well be that Buddhism, at least in Kerouac's writ-
ing, functions as a Catholic heresy. Kerouac certainly gives his bi-
ographers every reason to believe that he never for a moment
abandoned his Catholicism even though he never attended mass as
an adult. And some critics, like Kenneth Rexroth, certainly
doubted the validity of his understanding of Oriental scripture,
which he read only in translation. But the distinction Watts makes
brings up a problem worth contemplating: whether Kerouac sim-
ply used Buddhism to justify his lifestyle or whether he accorded
it full, independent authority as a belief system.

One sentence in Goddard's preface to *A Buddhist Bible*
strikes me as a possible explanation to this question and a key to
Kerouac's attraction to the book that provided him with his fun-
damental knowledge of three sutras. Goddard announces that the
book is not meant for scholarly purposes, but rather is "intended
to be a source of spiritual inspiration designed to awaken faith
and to develop faith into aspiration and full realization" (xv). Ker-
ouac carried this book with its avowedly devotional intent every-
where he went for several years, according to Nicosia. He even
carried it in a leather wrapper to a child support hearing in a New
York courtroom in January 1955 (Nicosia 471). I believe Kerouac
took the purpose of the book as his own purpose in reading it:
that is, his interest in Buddhism was genuinely spiritual, rather
than merely social. The three sutras in Goddard's collection—the
Diamond Sutra, the Surangama Sutra, and the Lankavatara Su-
tra—formed the textual basis for Kerouac's Buddhist devotions,
provided the philosophical ground of his Buddhist speculations,
and valorized the Buddhist vocabulary that gives power to his
poetry.

In Mahayana Buddhism Kerouac also found a fatalism that
corresponded to his own Celtic nostalgia, with the important dif-
ference that the inevitable extinction of the ego, instead of an
event to be feared, became the object and goal of his study and
meditation—and of his writing. Spengler (who was no fan of

Buddhism) embodied a similar fatalism, so Kerouac, in having read *The Decline of the West*, had previous experience of a profound resonance to this theme in a powerful text. Like *The Decline*, the Buddhist scriptures confirm the universality of two terms of the Kerouac family motto: work and suffer. Unlike Spengler's organic determinism, however, Buddhism makes a place for the third term: love. In fact, the impact of Buddha's Four Noble Truths—the omnipresence of suffering—is counterbalanced in Kerouac's writing only by the need for compassion. If suffering is life's given, the compassion for all sufferers must form the basis for an active response to human relations. In this sense, Kerouac's Buddhism might indeed be said to have provided him with an ethics.

"The theme of the Buddhist Bible," Goddard says, "is designed to show the unreality of all conceptions of a personal ego" (xvi). These words not only characterize the content of the book, but also the intellectual project of Kerouac's Buddhism as well. This project, I hasten to add, is neither negative nor self-destructive. It is a quest for a balanced way of being in the world. That is why Kerouac's father, Leo, takes on the character of the Ignorant Man, who knows his fate yet continues to live life moment by moment. In the end this man is the same as the one who ponders and rationalizes. The radical divisions in Kerouac's desire—between town life and city life, family and friends, past and present, solitude and fame—made it necessary for him to find a means of reconciling opposites. Buddhism served as that means. His attempt to eradicate his ego and the arbitrary conceptions of the world that flow from it created an allegory for the spiritual search for human unity. This allegory in *Mexico City Blues* takes the shape of a dialectic between Western words and Buddhist terminology with the effect, finally, that the terms neutralize each other, creating at least the linguistic illusion of balance, stability, unity.

Unity, of course, has literary as well as spiritual and psychological significance. There is really no way to know exactly how Kerouac felt when he wrote *Mexico City Blues*, and in some ways Kerouac's spiritual quest is just one more literary issue, available to readers only through other texts, such as biographies. The really pressing question is how his Buddhism functions in the poem to create a formal unity, one that can be perceived and experienced as unity by a compassionate reader. Kerouac's need was not unique, however. In his devotion to Buddhism, as in so many things, he seems to have captured the spirit of his age. *Mexico City Blues* is a profound cry uttered in behalf of American culture for meanings that our way of life—and therefore our individual ways of life—lacks. That is what gives the poem its power and living value.

Typically it is a tricky business to separate the work from the author and to separate both from the reader's interests. This difficulty is even more evident in Kerouac studies. If Kerouac was passing through Buddhism in the mid-1950s, he nevertheless remained a Catholic—for what that is worth—and sometimes his Buddhism sounds a great deal like Western philosophical idealism. It is impossible, of course, as Spengler insisted, for a person of one culture to understand the terms of another culture as the members of that culture understand them. Kerouac got his Buddhism in translation (this is Rexroth's criticism), but even a Westerner who can read Sanskrit, Pali, or Chinese is still translating the Buddhist terms into a Western mind. For literary purposes, it is of the utmost importance to understand how Buddhism functions as a trope in the poem, and it is best to treat Kerouac's Catholicism in the same manner—as a fund of images and a context for interpreting these images in his poetry.

To understand the precise quality of Kerouac's Catholicism is important in this context. His mother's devotion to "the Little Way" of St. Therese of Lisieux profoundly affected Kerouac's response to Catholicism and to religion in general. Mahayana Buddhism provided him with a conceptual order to balance against the mundane Catholic rituals he learned at home and in school as a child. As the complement to the ritualism of his family religion, he found himself drawn to an abstruse doctrine that required introspection, contemplation, and analysis. Memere's religion was mostly practice and little theory, while Kerouac's Buddhism appeared to many of his friends to be mostly theory and little practice.

If the two religions differ in Kerouac's usage—one outward in its orientation, the other inward—they are also similar in some respects. To Kerouac's mind Buddhism resembled his mother's peasant Catholicism because it also was a fellaheen religion. So, as different as Buddhism and Catholicism may be, Kerouac sets both together in contrast to the antireligious civilization of the city. In doing so, he is thinking like an orthodox Spenglerian despite that Spengler saw no analogy between Buddhism and Christianity. Kerouac repeatedly emphasized the religious meaning of the word *beat*, construing it to mean, among other things, *beatified*. This is the one sense in which he may be guilty of Watts's accusation: Kerouac's bohemianism involved a religious attitude toward life, an attitude he found lacking in mainstream culture. But his combination of Buddhism and Christianity results from an inner need, not a social rebellion. The literary precedent for his treatment of religion can be found in Yeats, who, also under the influence of Spengler, combined his native Protestantism with theosophical mysticism. Kerouac's quest, though very different in content from Yeats's, resembles it in one crucial respect: it represents an attempt to unify the poetic personality by providing it with a set of religious ideas complementary to those inculcated from birth. Whatever their personal value, these are precisely the kinds of ideas a writer needs to create dramatic tension in his works.

To say that the function of religion in Kerouac's works is primarily literary is not to deny the spiritual nature of his quest, for as Kerouac himself told poet Ted Berrigan in his *Paris Review* interview in reference to Yeats's automatic script: "Writing at least is a silent meditation" (68). Though that interview was conducted only two years before Kerouac's death, long after he had passed through Buddhism, it is still a valuable source of information about his spirituality. One of the things he makes clear, in his drunken, light-hearted, spontaneous way, is that he identified himself with the Buddha. "I am Buddha," he says outright, "and Ginsberg is Devadatta [Buddha's jealous cousin]" (87). When Berrigan asked Kerouac to explain the difference between Buddha and Jesus, he replied: "There is no difference" (87). Among other implications his response suggests the persistent theism of his religious thinking (Nicosia 494; Gifford and Lee 214). In the same part of the Berrigan interview, Kerouac asserts that "all I *write about* is Jesus," whereupon he identifies himself, in surreal fashion, as "Everhard Mercurian, General of the Jesuit Army" (85). While it is reasonable to accept this late self-assessment: "my serious Buddhism, that of ancient India, has influenced that part of my writing that you might call religious, or fervent, or pious, almost as much as Catholicism has" (Berrigan 85), it is also important to recognize that Buddhism had its greatest value in Kerouac's life and writing during the mid-1950s, a time when his age, his experience, and his art led him through a profound spiritual crisis.

Kerouac responded to that crisis by learning a new catechism, a set of dogmas with their appropriate terminology, and by identifying with a new hero: Buddha. In fact, he gave a sample of his biographical approach to Buddhism in the *Paris Review* interview, and it is apparent that in telling the story of the Buddha, he is also telling the story of his own life. The gist of it hinges on the importance of Buddha's discovery of the cause of death—a realization which plagued Kerouac's sexual life and became a major theme of *Mexico City Blues*. Though Kerouac's Catholicism was a given in his life (a terminus in either direction), his study of Buddhism was a voluntary act, but he uses both religions in the same way: he identifies with their founders, poeticizes their terminology, and extrapolates from them the few doctrines that correspond with his instinctive feelings—fatalism, compassion, attention, enlightenment, egolessness.

The human figures of both Catholicism and Buddhism—like the people in Kerouac's personal life—become characters in the drama of *Mexico City Blues*. The terms of the two doctrines line up in a complex imaginative dance. Compassion sets the tone of the poem—it is a mission of mercy to its readers. Extinction of the author's ego is the poem's goal. Kerouac's enlightenment, however, closely resembles Joyce's epiphany, and this similarity, like the precedent of Yeats, is a studied one. Satori consists (in the poem as in the later novel *Satori in Paris*) primarily in attention to and recognition of the quality of the thing perceived, whatever that quality may be. Further, Kerouac's identification with Jesus and Buddha was so complete, in the sense of negative capability, that the spiritual and literary dramas merge. The act of writing becomes contemplation; the act of living each moment fully becomes the practice of compassion. If I separate the literary from the spiritual in reading the poem, it is only for the sake of demonstrating their ultimate unity.

Nevertheless, Kerouac's alcoholism presents a formidable obstacle to perceiving this unity, which is often obscured by a boozy playfulness, as in the "209th Chorus":

> I got the woozes
> Said the wrong thing
> Want gold want gold
> Gold of eternity.

This is all too human for some readers, especially those who confuse spiritual search with Victorian earnestness, but booze or no, Kerouac at least intended to work out his spiritual values in his writing, and probably in his life as well.

The difference between the religion of the spontaneous poetry of *Mexico City Blues* and that of the antispontaneous *Scripture of the Golden Eternity* is the difference between practice and theory in ethics. One of the great attractions of *Mexico City Blues* is the way Catholic and Buddhist elements emerge, interact, and come into balance amid a distracting welter of other dramas. What drama one finds in the *Scripture* rests largely on the injunction in section 45: "When you've understood this scripture, throw it away. If you can't understand this scripture, throw it away. I insist on your freedom" (35). What Kerouac states aphoristically in the later work, he enacts in *Mexico City Blues*. A literary spirituality is by its very nature ambiguous because the author is striving, above all, to make it symbolic. So rather than proselytize, Kerouac the poet dramatizes his own unique spiritual evolution. The benefit to the reader lies not in some religious voyeurism, but in the opportunity to observe the details of that evolution in the process of becoming tropes.

The Buddhism of *Mexico City Blues*, I believe, like the Buddhism of *Tristessa* and *Visions of Gerard*, is a Buddhism in perfect equipoise with Catholicism. By contrast, the Buddhism of *The Dharma Bums*, written within two years of the poem, often seems preachy, even sappy. The Buddhism of *Mexico City Blues*, on the other hand, appears in its finest spiritual and literary bloom. In fact, it enlivens Kerouac's Catholicism, which was frequently so stale and dogmatic and is vibrant in the literary sense only in *Visions of Gerard*, another remarkable product of Kerouac's Buddhist period. Regardless of Kerouac's failure to build upon, solidify, practice, and renew his study during the last decade of his life, for a few years in the 1950s Buddhism became an agent of equilibrium in his life and clearly provided the direct impetus for him to become a poet. The openness of Kerouac's spiritual quest and his passion in the crisis of it are only the most immediate values of his religious poetry. The balance between the two religions—effectively a new religion, at once both private and public—helps make *Mexico City Blues* an extraordinary work of literature. In it, as in so much of Kerouac's fiction, the personal is transmuted into the representative, though the language of his poetry never loses its distinctive accent. Buddhism provided a counterbalance against Catholicism that allowed Kerouac to move forward into totally new fields of perception.

The historian Richard S. Sorrell has claimed that Kerouac's Catholicism was so much a part of his French-Canadian heritage that, like the French language of Kerouac's childhood, his religion became inextricable from his personality. While this may be a useful approach for the historian and the biographer who view the author as a product of his circumstances, I think it may be misleading to the reader of *Mexico City Blues*. And while it is accurate to say that Kerouac was a lifelong Catholic, it is unwise to underestimate the force of Buddhism in his middle career, a force at least temporarily as powerful as Catholicism. For the appreciative reader, the author is always productive of, as well as a product of, his times. In the literary sense Catholicism is simply a set of tropes with wide cultural significance, and the reader is left with the task of determining how this set functions in a particular work. Sorrell senses the arbitrariness of his own position, however, and incorporates a loophole into his argument: "The marginal ambivalence he [Kerouac] felt towards his confining ethnic past and the broader possibilities available in America produced an almost dual personality in Kerouac" (190). There is no "almost" about it; Catholicism and Buddhism stand for the dialectic of Kerouac's imagination. Catholicism represents the illiterate, philistine, lower-middle class of Kerouac's childhood, while Buddhism represents his aspirations toward the literate, middlebrow, upper-middle class. Catholicism conjures up images of Lowell; Buddhism calls forth images of New York City, California, and Mexico City. The best way to look at Catholicism in Kerouac's life, it seems to me, is as a form of excess, an imbalance that ultimately contributed to his premature demise.

There is something aesthetic about the counterweight of Kerouac's two religions, redolent of Aristotle's pity and terror. Spengler, in fact, found a similar pair in the origins of German Christianity; he called them *longing* and *dread*. "Fear God and love Him" Spengler believed to be the quintessential command of Western European religion (2:265). When Nicosia identifies Christianity in *Mexico City Blues* with "love of life" (481), he is sensing something of this distinction. It is obvious, though, that Buddhism, for Kerouac, calls up the emotion of compassion, while Catholicism connotes something more akin to safe haven—in other words, pity and terror. Buddhism is oriented toward this world, Catholicism toward the next. The two religions embody the elements of longing and dread, and one reason they function so well in tandem is that in this pair Kerouac made, as Charters says, "a discovery of different religious images for his fundamentally constant religious feelings" (190). The fundamental religious feelings in Kerouac's life and work are longing and dread, desire and death. For Kerouac this dialectic made living a constant agony, gave writing its infinite sense of drive, and cast a tone of nostalgia on the happiest scenes in both his life and his art.

"Any attempt to understand Kerouac's approach to writing," Nicosia says, "must take into account his deeply religious temperament" (326). I agree wholeheartedly; Jack Kerouac was that most elusive of all American creatures—an absolute individualist. He was born a Catholic yet never went to mass as an adult. He married three times, always in civil ceremonies. He discovered Buddhism, but as several of his friends testify, his Buddhism seemed always to have a theistic undertone (Gifford and Lee 214; Nicosia 494). The point is that Jack Kerouac was always religious, but never doctrinaire. The two established religions he favored were the language and imagery resources from which he constructed his own religion; they provided a means of expressing the profound and profoundly contradictory religious feelings he felt. For readers the issue is not one of belief but of performance. The question is how Kerouac's religious expression takes shape in the poem. Is it effective as expression?

In the final analysis, little can be learned from arguing whether Kerouac was a serious Buddhist or a devout Catholic. He was both and neither. He sought the middle path, his own path. "The idea of living religion," Nicosia notes, "was important to him, and where Buddhism diverged from common sense he repudiated it" (494). One may say precisely the same of Kerouac's Catholicism. Indeed, Kerouac once likened the Beats to a religious movement on the order of Taoism, Dionysism, and Buddhism, because they "strove to supplant the decadence of the technocracy" (McNally 237). He considered himself a pilgrim (Clark 81) and a part of a movement to bring religion back to the center of daily life. But more importantly, "Kerouac, as [his childhood friend] GJ later commented, made a religion out of whatever he was doing" (McNally 22). What he was doing, mainly, was writing, and the essential challenge of making a religious reading of *Mexico City Blues* lies in the attempt to separate Kerouac's religion from the established doctrines it derives from, while keeping firmly in mind that the poem itself, to his mind, embodied the ultimate religious act.

To narrow the discussion of Buddhism in the text of *Mexico City Blues* I will focus on three related topics: Kerouac's biographical interest in the Buddha, his commitment to compassion, and finally his development of the theme of anatta, or selflessness, in the poem. My knowledge of Buddhism is too limited to render judgment on the authenticity of Kerouac's interpretation of the sutras or the various doctrines they expound. To render the poem more accessible I will point out some connections and discuss possible interpretations of a few passages. I think it is safe to say that Buddhism represents the most dynamic theme in the poem. As Gary Snyder and others have observed, *Mexico City Blues* is primarily a religious poem. To understand it in terms of its Buddhist content, therefore, is to make an approach to the rationale of the poem itself. If it is effective as a religious poem, it must effectively—that is, movingly—enact its Buddhist content. My assumption is that *Mexico City Blues* is indeed successful in these terms: that it uses literary means to move the reader to the plane of spirituality.

The confessional nature of Kerouac's writing betrays a certain outlook on both art and life in which individual relations lie at the center of existence. Individuality supersedes ideology. The focus of life is on family and friends; the focus of art is on sensuous immediacy in time (as memory) and in space (as description). Kerouac's style, both personal and authorial, exudes this immediacy. It should come as no surprise, then, when I say that Kerouac's attraction to the Buddha was a personal one. "At the root of Kerouac's sudden fascination with Buddhism," Nicosia says, "may well have been an identification with the historic Buddha, Siddhartha Gautama" (457). The fact that Kerouac discovered Buddhism through Asvaghosa's early biography of the Buddha then went on to write his own version of the founder's life called *Wake Up!* (still unpublished) adds considerable weight to Nicosia's assertion. It is highly ironic that Kerouac applied his personal approach to Buddhism, since he uses the newfound doctrines primarily as an escape from personality. Nevertheless, this irony notwithstanding, it seems obvious that what Nicosia says is true. In fact, it may be an understatement. There is evidence in the poem, for instance, that more than simply identifying with the Buddha, Kerouac may have considered himself a reincarnation— another aspect of megalomania that, from an unsympathetic point of view, could be seen as a real flaw in aesthetic distance. To me, however, it seems perfectly valid to accept Kerouac's implicit belief that he—at least in the persona of the singer of *Mexico City Blues*—was indeed a bodhisattva, that is, an enlightened one who postponed nirvana to assist in the enlightenment of others. Accepting that mission of assistance is one way the poem moves from the literary to the spiritual.

The autobiographical element in *Mexico City Blues* (the Lowell Canto and a few other choruses) may itself be an imitation of Buddhist tradition. As in the Christian Gospels and Apocrypha, the Buddhist literature contains anecdotes and parables about the founder's life. One category of these tales is called *jataka*. The *jataka* are birth stories: parables of the Buddha's various reincarnations (Goddard 17, 21). In the Buddhist context, the entire Lowell Canto may be taken to represent a *jataka* in which we learn how the buddha Jack Kerouac started on his path to enlightenment. Even on a purely personal level, this may not be as pretentious as it sounds because Kerouac realized that the outcome of enlightenment was to resume a perfectly ordinary consciousness, as illustrated by the figure of the Ignorant Man in the poem. In addition, on a literary level, Kerouac hoped to demonstrate that one means of achieving egolessness is to transform the self into a trope.

Kerouac provides a number of explicit statements that strongly reinforce this notion of his identification with or reincarnation as the Buddha. Several choruses deal directly with Kerouac's mythic parentage. In the "69th Chorus," for example, he asks, "Who's my mother?" Two answers follow. First, the poet suggests that it "Goes back to Isis," meaning, I suppose, that relations among deities are somewhat ambiguous, and more pointedly that the mother/sister of the slain and resurrected god is not only the prototype of the Blessed Virgin but also the prototype of Kerouac's mother—perhaps of all mothers. He proceeds to identify himself with Christ, who universalized his relationship to make himself blood kin to all of humanity. Christ and Buddha are merged to a large extent in the poem, specifically in the "24th Chorus," and generally in the "21st," "148th," and "226th" choruses. When Kerouac identifies with Christ, he is identifying by analogy with Buddha. He considers himself both a saint and a bodhisattva—in either case, one who is on a mission of mercy to the human race. He feels sufficiently justified in this belief to address the readers/listeners of the "68th Chorus" as "my disciples of the modern world."

The issue of Kerouac's lineage recurs in two later choruses where he again raises the question of motherhood. In the "225th Chorus," after introducing her on the previous page, he begins a paean to Damema, the wife of the Tibetan sage Milarepa. The singer describes his spiritual quest here:

117

> I keep restless mental searching
> And geographical meandering
> To find the Holy Inside Milk
> Damema gave to all.

The implication is that he is one of the sons of Damema, but in a sense, so are we all. He addresses her by her traditional epithet, "Mother of Buddhas," and ascribes to her the origin of milk, which signifies compassion as well as motherhood.

After a dozen choruses in which the singer tries to resolve all of the various Buddhist themes he has introduced in the course of the poem—with the conclusion "No Self God Heaven" ("232nd Chorus")—he returns to Damema. The "237th Chorus" begins with the statement in French: "My mother, you are the earth." Here *ma mere* is a pun on Kerouac's mother's nickname. "What does that mean?" the singer asks. "For one thing, Damema was the mother of Buddhas." The inference that he identifies his own mother with Damema seems inescapable. The description of the veneration of the Blessed Virgin that follows, which is repeated precisely in *Tristessa* (11, 30), underscores the similarity between Damema and Mary, who has already been identified with Isis. In *Tristessa*, the narrator recognizes that Damema is an anagram for *ma Dame*, the traditional French form of address for the Virgin. To add to the multiple identification, McNally says that Kerouac equated Damema with Esperanza Villanueva, the model for the character of Tristessa, and also, even though Esperanza was a prostitute and sterile, that she represented motherhood in his mind (196).

To conclude the chorus, the singer compares Damema with the Virgin, then mentions Maya, the mother of the historical Buddha. The final theme here is the death of the mother. According to Asvaghosa, Damema died from joy after her newborn son was visited by several sages. Likewise, Maya died a week after giving birth to Sakyamuni. Mary, of course, did not die, but survived Jesus to be assumed into heaven alive. Kerouac's mother also survived him, so it seems somewhat odd that the singer here extols the mythic mothers for "Going to heaven on their impulse / Pure and free and champion of birth." Again, the implication is that

Kerouac, or at least the singer, conceives of himself as the son of one or all of these mythic mothers. To certify his affiliation and allegiance he dedicates the poem to Damema, whom he calls, perhaps in reflection of Ginsberg's similar gesture to Neal Cassady in "Howl," "the Secret Hero." This designation comes immediately before the Charlie Parker choruses and the close of the poem as the finale to the Buddhist theme. Damema is the secret hero of the poem because she has given birth to the line of Buddhas—including Kerouac himself—and also because she has given birth to compassion in the heart of the singer of the poem.

Earlier, in the "111th Chorus," the singer had described his enlightenment as simply "dropping all false conceptions." After doing so, he says, he "turned to the world, / a Buddha inside." This inner Buddha is nourished by Damema's "Holy Inside Milk" ("225th Chorus"). It gives the singer courage for the quest, courage to say to the "Saints of McCarthy" in the "125th Chorus":

> remove my name
> from the list
> And Buddha's too
> Buddha's me, in the list,
> no-name.

It gives him the authority to speak, in the "182nd Chorus," "As a Buddha." Finally, it allows him to canonize himself, in both the Catholic and Buddhist senses, and to call himself, near the end of the poem, "The Venerable Kerouac, friend of Cows" ("216th-B Chorus"). The singer's memory of birth into this life ("140th Chorus") and of existence in a previous life ("127th Chorus") both suggest the fully awakened condition of a Buddha.

In a rush to render the obvious Oedipal version of Kerouac's relationship with his mother it would be easy to miss the religious implications of divine motherhood. It seems clear that Kerouac is telling his own story as a parable of englightenment. He has become a bodhisattva, rendering his service to humankind before attaining parinirvana, the stage at which he will finally escape the cycle of rebirths entirely. His mother, it appears, is more than his mother—and less. Kerouac senses that Memere is both a personal and a universal mother. Like the other mythic mothers, she has begun a lineage of Buddhas—in this case, all of Kerouac's disciples who achieve enlightenment. Not only does maternity determine the singer's personal perspective on Buddhism, but it also adds a unique universal dimension to Kerouac's reading of Buddhism, an innovative Catholic emphasis on the origin of the founder of Kerouac's adopted religion.

The milk of motherhood, Damema's "Holy Inside Milk," also calls to mind the milk of human kindness. Kerouac's favorite Buddhist saint was Avalokitesvara, the bodhisattva of compassion. The notion of a man who defers nirvana for the sake of showing kindness to his fellow beings stirred his religious imagination. The importance of compassion suffuses the writing Kerouac did in 1955 and 1956. The second part of *Tristessa*, for instance, revolves around the narrator's sympathy for the protagonist's fallen human condition. Likewise, *Visions of Gerard* paints the portrait of Kerouac's older brother as a young Saint Francis (Gerard's patron saint), the Catholic equivalent of Avalokitesvara. Describing Kerouac's state of mind in Mexico in August 1955, when he was writing *Mexico City Blues*, Nicosia says, "Kerouac's motto was 'Conscious continual compassion and ordinary contentedness . . . simple kicks'" (476). As a part of his study of Buddhism, Kerouac enquired deeply into the nature of compassion, and his enquiry led him to dedicate his long poem as a mission of mercy to his readers.

This mission is announced in a highly significant pun in the "1st Chorus," which ends with the line "Mersion of Missy." This seems to allude to Kerouac's attempt to abstain from sex (a "submersion" or repression of women, "Missy"), or in general, the effort to escape desire. The connection of desire and compassion comes from Kerouac's interpretation of Buddha's Four Noble Truths. Suffering is the fundamental truth, and suffering follows from desire. If desire is stilled, then suffering ceases. One role of the bodhisattva of compassion, then, is to show others how to escape desire and thus eliminate suffering. Kerouac adds a new twist to the discussion of compassion, however, by including himself as a potential object of his own compassion. If he is to practice mercy towards others, he realizes, he must practice it toward himself as well. Coming from a self-destructive individual, this sounds especially poignant. In one sense, then, *Mexico City Blues* is a didactic poem. It tries to show its reader/listener how to eliminate suffering. "Emancipate the human masses / Of this world from slavery to life / And death," the singer sings in the "216th-B Chorus." "O Samson me that," he thinks to add, mindful of the difficulty of his task.

The vehicle mentioned in the "1st Chorus" is Mahayana Buddhism (the term literally means "the great vehicle"), but Kerouac also invents a ship to sail through the poem. At first called the "S. S. Excalibur"—a name that apparently came to him in a dream (*Book of Dreams* 56)—in honor of the sword that brought the benevolent King Arthur to power in the romantic legend, the ship ends up with the name "*SS Mainline*" in the "229th Chorus." By this time, it has become a "Fishin Ship," with all the appropriate Christian connotations of fishing. We learn that it is "reeling in the merit like mad." "Mainline" refers both to drug use and to railroading. In one sense, the ship will serve as an opiate to deaden suffering, while in another sense, it will carry those it has rescued on the most direct route to enlightenment.

The route to Kerouac's own enlightenment led him to compose an anti-sonnet called the "Art of Kindness" ("20th Chorus), and his singer asserts at one point that he has "eyes of Avalokitesvara" ("60th Chorus"). He reminds himself and others: "don't break your tenderness" ("122nd Chorus"). The object of these utterances is to raise compassion closer to the surface of everyday awareness. The climactic chorus for the theme of compassion comes in the singer's repetition of the "Art of Kindness" in the "157th Chorus." Here we get compassion within a strictly Buddhist framework. Despite the singer's recognition of the arbitrariness of conceptions of lover and beloved as subject and object, he nevertheless espouses "the Single Teaching: Love Everywhere." Compassion becomes "Love of Objectlessness." Returning in the "169th Chorus" to the association between compassion and sexual desire, the singer advises his listeners to "forgive, reassure, pat, protect, / and purify" the living in "whatever way is best." He attributes this injunction to the Tathagata (an epithet for a fully enlightened Buddha).

The "60th Chorus" presents an interesting example of the practice of compassion in the text. This chorus concerns Kerouac's perception that he had been wronged by his friend John Clellon Holmes, who, Kerouac believed, had cribbed much of his fictional material. The singer confronts his own anger over Holmes's financial gain in the middle stanza of the chorus:

> It means that I have been asked
> To receive a brother
> Who sinned against me
> And I knew all the time
> The saints were for me.

He provides this as an example of the practice of compassion, as an application of the admonition in the "123rd Chorus": "Forgive everyone for yr own sins / And be sure to tell them / You love them which you do." Having learned to forgive others, the singer is now ready to forgive himself, or at least to provide for his own forgiveness.

"Tryin to figure yr way / outa the calamity of dust and eternity," he recognizes in the "119th Chorus," "you better / get on back to your kind / boat." In a Buddhist context, compassion for others is necessary to Kerouac's quest, but he is also led to the realization that he, too, needs compassion. First, inverting the pun of the "1st Chorus," he asks for "Mercy on Mission" ("128th Chorus"). Then he questions the origin of blame in the "178th Chorus," asking, "Who put the blame? / Who's trying to throw me out?" Because he suffers pain, he knows others suffer pain. Because he feels compassion for others who suffer, he discovers that he deserves compassion for the pain he himself suffers. He learns by introspection that the Buddhist saints have escaped suffering by recognizing that the essence of existence is void. In the "188th Chorus," he implores them to guide him to a similar realization:

> O bless me, make me safe,
> say, 'No-Yo' but save
> 'Me no?' save

No-me—I beseech
save no-me.

Compassion involves not only the attempt to escape desire, but
since this attempt depends on abolishing the arbitrary concept of
the self, compassion also involves the irony of asking salvation for
a self that does not exist.

The most overwhelming expression of suffering occurs in the
paired "211th" and "212th" choruses. "All this meat is in dreadful
pain," the "212th Chorus" begins. The preceding chorus, which
Charters calls "perhaps the most eloquent poem in the book"
(228), concludes with an expression of a wish for compassion that
combines Buddhist and Christian imagery: "*Poor!* I wish I was
free / of that slaving meat wheel / and safe in heaven dead." Fi-
nally, the singer concludes that to be worthy of compassion, he
must still even the desire for compassion: "I'm completely in
pain," he says, "Waiting without mercy / For the worst to hap-
pen" ("227th Chorus"). With this stilling of desire, he sees that
the Buddhist saints possess "perfect compassionate pity / Without
making one false move / of action" ("236th Chorus"). In closing
the poem, he aligns himself with this Buddhist attitude, which he
describes as "Perfectly accommodating commiserations / For all
sentient belaboring things."

Now he is ready to transfer the responsibility for removing
the burden of guilt and suffering to a contemporary American in-
carnation of the Buddha, bop saxophonist Charlie Parker. The
role of Parker becomes clear in this context. He is not the hero of
the poem; rather, he is a bodhisattva to be invoked as a way of
concluding the poem. The message of Bird's music is the same as
the message of Gerard's dream: "All is Well." By recognizing in
Parker a being with a mission identical to his own, Kerouac is
able, finally, to beg forgiveness. In the process the musician him-
self is utterly transformed (see "241st Chorus"), and by a transmu-
tation of sounds, the "Mersion of Missy" becomes "merit / Not to
be measured" as the deferred enlightenment of these bodhisattvas
is applied to the salvation of other sentient beings. The singer's
last request is for compassion for himself and for all of humanity.
By losing himself in the quest, he is able to put himself in the po-

sition of those he has vowed to help. The distinction between subject and object has all but disappeared. What others require, the singer also requires. What he requires, he now knows, is exactly the compassion he has sworn to feel for others. "Charley Parker," he begs, "lay the bane, / off me, and every body."

If Kerouac identified with the historical Buddha on the personal level and strove to understand and exercise compassion on the practical level, he found that on the theoretical level his most formidable task was to analyze and internalize the concept of annata, or no soul. Since Goddard had stated in *A Buddhist Bible* that this doctrine was the gist of all the texts he included in the book, Kerouac wanted to explore its ramifications in great detail. In *Mexico City Blues* this exploration focuses on two related issues: first, the emptiness of all forms, both mental and material; second, the need to neutralize one's selfhood to escape suffering. Kerouac realized that compassion was only a stopgap to alleviate suffering; the only way to eliminate it entirely was to eliminate its cause. Both the emptiness of form and the nonexistence of the ego can be approached by examining "arbitrary conceptions." Once the seeker recognizes that all distinctions are pretty much conventional, he or she gains access to the truth that the "essence of emptiness / is essence of gold" ("105th Chorus"). This is the main argument of the poem, and I want to trace its development both in explicit terms and in terms of the image most closely associated with it: balloons.

The kernel of the spiritual drama in the poem is contained between the "182nd" and the "205th" choruses, a section I call the Essence of Existence Canto. Here the singer combines the doctrines of Buddhism, allusions to its great teachers, and quotations from its sacred texts with his own personal reflections. He even includes a prayer for the emancipation of all sentient beings. Set forth in this canto are the themes of the singer's quest: the acceptance of the emptiness of reality, the attempt to escape the bondage of the self, the need for compassion, and the reward of attaining an awareness of Universal Mind. In the course of these twenty-four choruses, the singer achieves release from suffering and simultaneously learns how to compose his songs spontaneously. At the conclusion of the canto, just before he begins the finale of the entire poem, the singer enters "the Holy Stream" to "March with the Saints" and "Follow along the emptiness" ("205th Chorus").

Mexico City Blues actually begins with a formal statement of the doctrine of the emptiness of form: "Butte Magic / Is the same as no-Butte" ("1st Chorus"), and then a few lines later: "Denver is the same." The town of Butte, Montana, holds great significance in Kerouac's mythography. Not only does it lie near the source of the Missouri River, which flows into the Mississippi, signifying both the span of the continent and its division into East and West, but it is also the home of Doctor Sax (*Dr. Sax* 29) and Bull Balloon (*Visions of Gerard* 113), two cartoon-like characters who crusade against evil in Kerouac's fiction. In general for Kerouac, towns like Butte and Denver stand for freedom, individuality, and heroism, so when he negates them at the outset of *Mexico City Blues* he makes a sweeping statement about his own legend, the Legend of Duluoz, as well as the nature of the world.

The key to understanding the doctrine of the emptiness of form lies in the concept of "arbitrary conceptions." The singer of the poem takes up this term, adopted from the sutras, in the "7th Chorus." Here, continuing his discussion from the previous chorus, he lists a series of epithets for the Tathagata, the fully enlightened one. The one that begins this chorus is "He Who is Free From Arbitrary Conceptions / of Being or Non-Being." Already, the singer is trying to find the middle path—that is, the way that runs between the polarities of thought and language. When he takes up this theme again in the "108th Chorus," he explains his position clearly:

> arbitrary conceptions
> have sprung into existence
> that didnt have to be there
> in the first place.

Instead of seeing the void, human beings, because of the accumulated action of the senses, and especially because of language, see forms that delude us with desire and distract us from the ultimate knowledge of reality.

In investigating arbitrary conceptions, Kerouac comes squarely up against the dilemma of the role of language. As a poet he is forced to admit that the very medium of his expression contributes to the illusion created by arbitrary conceptions. He images words as a cartoonist like Thurber would: he puts them in a balloon. In the "109th Chorus" he calls the cartoon balloon a "WORD - HOLE," introducing the Spenglerian notion that words occur in strictly circumscribed contexts and carry thoroughly transitory meanings. He follows out the implications of this notion in the very poignant "118th Chorus."

Here the singer explains how, having accepted the arbitrariness of words, he can still justify making poems. He admits the value of words as indicators leading to the truth that form is void, but he rejects that they have any substance in religious terms. "I've had times of no-singing," he says; "they were the same [as the times of singing] / Music is noise, Poetry dirt." In his spiritual quest the poet must relinquish even his dependence on words because they are simply pointers with which he is able to write "a nothing poem / no-poem non poem" ("202nd Chorus") and ultimately to say, as the singer of *Mexico City Blues* says, "I don't even exist less sing" ("227th Chorus"). The words of the poem become the pointers that lead the spirit away from the illusion of the forms they help create toward the realization that words, above all, exemplify the arbitrary conceptions that mask the void that is existence. This is the kind of knowledge that the poet knows best.

Ignorance, Buddhism teaches, is the cause of the illusion of arbitrary conceptions. Somewhat like the prisoners in Plato's cave, humans deluded by form have only to turn away from it toward the source of the mutable world in order to escape their delusion. Kerouac proposes that poetry can use words to turn the tables on themselves: "An asinine form," he describes it in the "85th Chorus," "which will end / all asininity / from now on." He draws a similar lesson from one of Garver's dreams, which teaches him that "the essence does not pass / From mouth to mouth" but that "ignorance does. / ignorant form" ("165th Chorus"). Both poetry and dreams offer insight into the insubstantiality of form and therefore provide means to escape from the slavery of ignorance, the "multiple too-much of the world" ("175th Chorus").

In the "176th Chorus" the singer summarizes his position on arbitrary conceptions: "The reasons why there are so many things / Is because the mind breaks it up." Only a buddha can draw attention to the emptiness of forms and teach "what it means / For there to be too many things / In a world of no-thing." Kerouac formulates an equation from his awareness: "One no-thing / Equals / All things." This state of awareness is called "Universal Mind," and those who attain it

> accept everything,
> see everything,
> it is empty,
> Accept as thus — the Truth. ("183rd Chorus")

The awareness of Universal Mind yields a release from fear, especially fear of death. To conclude his exploration of this theme, the singer quotes from the sutras:

> "the void
> is not really void
> but the real realm
> of the Dharma"—.   ("184th Chorus")

"Dharma" for Kerouac means the self-regulating power of the universe (Gifford and Lee 14), so the awareness of emptiness renders a kind of equilibrium within and without, and the seeker who attains it gains a sense of resignation about the strife between good and evil in the world. This resignation—not quietism or passivity—is the goal of the Buddhist search, and one of the primary purposes of *Mexico City Blues* is to help the readers to acquire it.

From the view that the world of forms is an empty world, it follows that the creator of these forms, the individual ego, is also empty. The quest, consequently, necessitates the deconstruction of individual identity: the annihilation—or neutralization—of the self. Discussing this process in Buddhist doctrine, Goddard explains that "when the ego discerned its immaterial nature, it would attain true deliverance" (7). One of the texts he includes in *A Buddhist Bible* assures the reader that "only terrestrial human beings think of selfhood as being a personal possession" (92). So the second part of the theme of no-soul in *Mexico City Blues* involves the singer's attempt to explain the method and advantages of achieving selflessness. This part of the theme, like the first part, is stated early in the poem, but it is worked out in great detail only in the later choruses, and the finale of the poem gains most of its momentum from the singer's insistence on the abandonment of the self.

It may seem paradoxical that an avowedly autobiographical writer like Jack Kerouac would choose for the main theme of his major poem the annihilation of the self. The Duluoz Legend, to be sure, is a carefully conceived plan to create a complete fictional version of the self. Kerouac's style is rich in markers of personality. The man himself was a notorious character, a human personality valued for its own sake. Perhaps through Buddhism Kerouac came to realize just how overwhelmingly self-centered his life was. Something ascetic lies in his notion of the abandonment of self, as though, as a penance, he was willing to give up the most important thing in his life. He recognized, however, that his ego had caused him much pain. As a writer he sensed more easily than others what an artificial creation one's personality really is. Through his fiction he learned how characters are constructed and what degree of negative capability is required of the artist to create credible fictional personalities. In *Mexico City Blues* he carries his fictionalization of himself onto a religious plane by attempting to create a self that dissolves.

His treatment of the Lowell Canto reinforces my supposition. After some fifteen choruses of autobiography, in which he has given his family a purposefully mythic quality, his transition back into the stream of the poem deals directly with the issue of no-soul. "Man," the singer asserts, "is the same as man, / The same as no-man, the same / As Anyman, Everyman" ("105th Chorus"). The middle path for the poet is the universalization of the self, a kind of simultaneous transmutation and loss. What could be better for an artist than to find a religion that sanctions the abandonment of the self to emphasize the arbitrariness of form? The chorus form in *Mexico City Blues* joins repetition and innovation in a tension designed to embody the universal and unique aspects of selfhood. The self that exists in the poem proves that the self writing the poem is not a fixed entity but a flow and flux that exists only by inference from its creations. The autobiography exists only as it is written. Nothing is more thoroughly fictional than the fiction of the self.

In order to deconstruct his self, Kerouac must investigate the nature of memory, and this leads him to muse on the reality of time. At the close of the Lowell Canto, the singer concludes:

> My remembrance of my father
> . . . .
> is the same empty material
> as my father in the grave. ("103rd Chorus")

His past is implicated in the illusion of the solidity of self, and to escape from self, he must abandon any notion that his memories demonstrate the persistence, coherence, or continuity of the self. After mulling over the implications of this discovery, the singer makes a pronouncement much later in the poem in the "204th Chorus," one of the most elegant choruses in the book. Here, he tells us that "Time is dust," that it's "already happened / immemorially," with a heavy pun on this last word. The singer concludes the chorus with a continuation of the question and answer format:

> What's been buried inside me
>   for sure?
> The substance of my own father's
>   empty light
> Derived from time working
>   on dirt
> And clay bones.
>   Buddha's River.

Having learned by contemplating the sutras, Kerouac is able to internalize the meaning of emptiness. His father—the image of Ignorant Man—has led him to the awareness of emptiness. Substantial flesh turns out to be insubstantial, and Kerouac's patrimony comes in the form of enlightenment, the release from self. "Don't worry bout time," he hears his singer sing.

This part of the theme is actually introduced in the "6th Chorus," where the singer paraphrases the conclusion of the Diamond Sutra (Goddard 106). One short stanza is all the singer needs to set forth the entire doctrine:

> Self depends on existence of other
> self, and so no Solo Universal Self
> exists—no self, no other self,
> no innumerable selves, no
> Universal self and no ideas
> relating to existence or non-
> existence thereof—.

Then, having set forth the doctrine, he suggests a method of practicing it. The

> radiant irradiation
> From middleless center
> . . . .
> Is not Owned by Self-Owner
> but found by Self-Loser—.   ("25th Chorus")

The purpose of the remainder of the poem will be to develop an effective poetic way to lose the self.

From the "129th Chorus," where the singer avers that in life "The Victor is Not Self," to the "167th Chorus," with its wonderful characterization of selflessness, "Beginningless Ecstatic Nobody," the poem builds its argument and signals its stress on the annihilation of the self. The theme permutes into a litany that seems calculated, like a mantra, to facilitate release. The long second stanza of the "185th Chorus" rises with the chant "No-self, no-self, no-self," which is followed by the entreaty "No-me—I beseech / save no-me" ("188th Chorus"). The prayer contained in the "192nd" and "193rd" choruses is uttered in behalf of "all /

who are in bondage to self." This frenzy leads directly to the connection between loss of self and compassion in the "194th Chorus":

> Being in selfless one-ness
> With the such-ness
> That is Tathagatahood,
> So is everybody else
> Lost with you
> In that bright sea
> Of non-personality.

As it turns out, the singer discovers, loss of self creates a sense of human community because the self-loser recognizes his or her similarity both to the principle of suchness, tathata, and to the struggle with personality in which all people are engaged.

What follows betokens true release from self, full awareness, complete enlightenment. The singer articulates his conviction that any quest conducted in the name of personal identity is worthless. One difference between heaven and nirvana, for instance, is that no self is translated safely into an afterlife. Neither is nirvana within oneself because there is no self ("198th Chorus"). This issue becomes the object of intense speculation in the "218th Chorus": "I wanta go to Inside-Me, / Is there such a place? No is." But this negation smacks too much of arbitrary conception, of the polarity of rational thought, so it must be modified. This modification occurs immediately in the following chorus, in a setting from Doestoevsky's classic novel *The Brothers Karamazov*, in answer to a battery of questions:

> No me? No drama to desire?
> . . . .
> No saints? . . .
> No no? . . .

The singer's answer is this marvelous locution from the firm ground of the middle path: "No such thing as no." What a profound yet playful affirmation coaxed from the resources of language and poetic form!

After this the counters all fall into place. The past has no claim on self, because "All has been done" ("224th Chorus"). Sleep bears witness to the inherent value of selflessness by reminding us nightly of "the void that's highly embraceable" ("225th Chorus"). Independent of notions of the self, the seeker finds that there is "no way to lose" ("226th Chorus"). At this point the singer also escapes from bondage to the poetic self: "I don't even exist less sing" ("227th Chorus"). He concludes that there is "no self God heaven" ("232nd Chorus"). The lack of punctuation in the series appears to indicate the identity of the elements in the singer's mind.

The grand finale occurs in the "233rd Chorus," a chorus that ends where it begins: "There is no selfhood that can begin the practice / of seeking to attain." This is a direct quote from the Diamond Sutra, Kerouac's favorite Buddhist text (Goddard 98), and it is obviously intended to be the final word on the subject. Case closed. Only the practical application of the loss of self remains to be demonstrated, and given Kerouac's obsessions, it has to do with death. It is also oddly ambiguous. "But it's hard to pretend you dont know," the singer intones, "That when you die you wont know" ("235th Chorus"). It sounds as though the escape from self makes the fear of death a game he is playing with himself. The assurance of no-self is so strong that his fear of losing his personal identity through death seems like some sort of bizarre superstition. He is beyond the arbitrary conceptions of self and no-self at this point, and the dialectic has ceased to matter. He is living fully in the present: "How do I know that I'm dead. / Because I'm alive / and I got work to do."

The singer has joined the "bright confraternity" of the bodhisattvas by escaping the "mutual dual twin opposites" of life and death. He has experienced "the central / lapse and absence of them both" ("236th Chorus") and finds himself, very near the end of his song, reposing in "Love's Holy Void Abode." He has played out the theme of no-soul successfully, and his transition into everyday consciousness, following his progress from the problematics of personality, family, history, and time, seems remarkably sure. He is ready to end the poem with his invocation to Charlie Parker, and the final chorus, with its transcendental sound of silence, has the tone of a disembodied spirit—it is neither the self of Jack Kerouac the writer nor the self of the singer whose familiar inflections have guided the listener through the maze of themes in the poem. In the end, *Mexico City Blues* proves to be a poem that enacts no-soul. It quashes its own argument in favor of an object lesson in how to escape the self.

Another important aspect to be discussed is the imagery associated with the doctrine of no-soul. Every good poem presents an effective balance of sound and sight, so it is especially worthwhile to explain how a fundamentally oral poet like Kerouac manipulates one of his central images. If the *oo* sound is the most important sound in *Mexico City Blues* and no-soul its most important theme, the balloon is the poem's most important image. It is the perfect commonplace to represent the doctrine of no-soul: simple, colorful, redolent of childhood, accessible through the experience of each and all. Kerouac's handling of the image, moreover, is no less masterful than his inception of it.

In conversation in 1988, Allen Ginsberg told me that Kerouac picked up the balloon image in the early 1950s from a Hungarian woman who was, at the time, the lover of writer Alan Harrington. They had all gone together to a party at an apartment filled with balloons. The Hungarian woman made such a big deal out of the balloons, repeating the word itself with such childlike wonder, that Kerouac never forgot the impression. But besides the autobiographical origin, the image of balloons also has its origins in one of the Hindu symbols of emptiness, "bubbles on the Ganges" (Goddard 27). In fact, the singer uses this image early in the poem (in the "10th" and "24th" choruses) to characterize human insignificance. It also incorporates the *oo* sound, so that in performing the poem even the singer's mouth makes the shape that signifies emptiness. But the first mention of balloons, in the "27th Chorus," comes with a surprising fullness that foreshadows the finale of the poem. The conclusion to this "Vast Integral Crap / a / Balloons" is: "BALLOONS is your time / B a l l o o n s is the ending / THAT'S THE SCENE." Unless the reader is aware of the connection between the image and the theme and also of the importance of the theme itself, this chorus will likely seem extravagant. In the context of Kerouac's investigation of no-soul, however, it stands as one of the most important landmarks in *Mexico City Blues.*

"One of Kerouac's means of conveying emptiness," Nicosia says, "is to show each thought form as a 'balloon' lost in space, an idea he and Allen got from the balloon-enclosed dialogue in comic strips" (483). The relation between the cartoon balloon and the doctrine of no-soul is made explicit in the "109th Chorus" in the setting of a Thurber drawing. Here the balloon appears to be bursting—"ball / OON LINE ANOON / POP CLOUD - WORD - HOLE"—so even the line that circumscribes the words and ties them to the character that utters them disappears. The balloon becomes, for the poet, a word hole that swallows up his intentions and dispels the illusion of permanence in meaning.

This cartoon aspect of the balloon image extends into the metaphysics of no-soul, as well. One of the most innovative choruses in *Mexico City Blues* is the "41st," where the singer discusses the structure of the mind. He represents the mind in two ways: first as a word with a large gap between its third and fourth letters, next as an oval with "Nothing" inscribed within. In addition to reading the line across—"In the min d's central comedy"—it must also be read down—"In the min / (ute and long ago lament) / of mind's central comedy." An arrow also runs from the gap in the word toward the inscribed oval, indicating that the content of the signifier and signified is both "Nothing" and nothing, a stunningly imaginative way of representing the analysis as a product of arbitrary conceptions. The last word in this chorus, which stands in apposition to the phrase, "mind's central / comedy," is "BAL-LOONS." This conclusion suggests that the ultimate image of mind, as of emptiness or no-soul, can be summed up in a balloon.

When the balloon occurs in other choruses, it contributes a certain gaiety to whatever notion it is related to, a gaiety born of conviction. In the "99th Chorus," for instance, Kerouac's father, Leo, comes across as a kind of Major Hoople. His face and eyes, as well as the sounds he makes, resemble "'big burper balloons / of the huge world'." As the figure of Ignorant Man, Leo does not know that he represents emptiness, but his not knowing is itself a better proof of emptiness than the enlightened person's knowing. The singer brings paternity into the proper relation with the doctrine of no-soul through the balloon image. Likewise, in the "183rd Chorus," he invents the amusing image of the Chinese sage who "Had eyes to see the Karma / Wobbling in the balloon." In both cases, the playfulness of the balloon—its association with childhood—invests the treatment of the doctrine with humor. This humor, in turn, dispels the lugubrious tone that might otherwise turn the poem into preachment or proselytizing.

The last mention of balloons in *Mexico City Blues* comes in the "199th Chorus," which commands the reader to "S w e a r" by a series of examples of emptiness. The chorus begins with this question: "Empty balloons of gorgeous?" Since by this point the singer has attained a true appreciation of no-soul, the appropriate answer is neither yes nor no. The balloons can only be discerned by one who has not yet learned the emptiness of form. In fact, by this time the singer has fallen into the space hole ("191st Chorus"), which is related to the word hole of the "109th Chorus" and perhaps to what is depicted in the "41st Chorus." This space hole, the void occupied by the self of the singer and the self writing the poem, Kerouac declares, is "my startingplace and my goal." The singer formulates this matter-of-fact proposition to describe his realization that emptiness means merely finding out what, in your heart of hearts, you already knew.

From this source spring the fount of ordinary awareness and the stream of human compassion, as well as the words and images of poetry, the medium that allows Kerouac to create a singing self with which to dismantle his other self. This is the poetry of the sutras; the words are likened to fingers pointing at the truth: don't get hung up on the fingers. The doctrine of no-soul in *Mexico City Blues* illustrates perfectly that saying of Neal Cassady's: "Lyric is supported on bubbles and what is too foolish to be said is sung" (Charters 165). By singing no-self Kerouac manages to present the doctrine as he understands it, and his performance enables the audience to experience it. Best of all, when the singing is done, in the final chorus, after all the bright balloons have floated out of sight into the sky, we see only the emptiness of form, hear only the silence of the void.

7

The Tradition of Spontaneity

The supposedly single, independent and external world that each believes to be common to all is really an ever-new, uniquely occurring and non-recurring experience in the existence of each.

In the "Passing Through New York" section of *Desolation Angels*, Kerouac invents a fictional version of an actual meeting he had with the New Critic and poet Randall Jarrell in the presence of Gregory Corso. Varnum Random, the Jarrell character, asks Duluoz, the Kerouac character, "How can you get any refined or well gestated thoughts into a spontaneous flow as you call it? It can all end up gibberish" (280).

Duluoz, who has just finished writing a series of poems "high on benny in the parlor," defends his "theory of absolute spontaneity" by replying:

> "If it's gibberish, it's gibberish. There's a certain amount of control going on like a man telling a story in a bar without interruptions or even one pause."
>
> "Well it'll probably become a popular gimmick but I prefer to look upon my poetry as craft," Random says.

"Craft *is* craft."

"Yes? Meaning?"

"Meaning crafty. How can you confess your crafty soul in craft?" (280)

As this passage amply illustrates, Kerouac's notion of spontaneity, despite the adjective, is neither absolute nor strictly poetic. It admits a measure of control, and its purpose seems partly artistic, partly religious, and partly personal. While no facet of literary aesthetics has been more thoroughly ignored, the theory and practice of spontaneity form the foundation for most of Kerouac's novels (with the possible exception of *The Town and the City*) and command special prominence in the composition and content of his poetry. Because spontaneity often misleadingly implies the most radical originality—often the illusion of creation out of thin air—I choose to view it in terms of its various sources in Kerouac's life and work. That he worked self-consciously within a tradition makes his spontaneous poetics all the more impressive and important. Tradition, after all, distinguishes literature from the rest of imaginative writing, and in no way does working within a tradition of spontaneity diminish Kerouac's originality or authority. The most productive way to treat Kerouac's poetics is to view him as a great innovator in a long line of eminent writers.

Besides the indefinable boundary between poetry and prose, the most ancient distinction in literature is between the epic poem and the lyric poem, the poem that tells the hero's story as opposed to the poem that is, as Wallace Stevens put it, "the cry of its occasion." These fundamental genres can be recognized by length, structure, and conventions, of course, but they can also be said to employ different approaches to spontaneity. In the epic poem, the story comes almost ready-made from the resources of the culture; it is mythic and almost prerational in nature. The hero and the other characters in the story are well-known to the listeners. Even many of the details of plot and setting are dictated by convention. Yet an element of spontaneity remains. We know that in oral literatures the singer of the epic uses the elaborate structure of the poem as a foundation for freedom of style. Because the content of the poem is restricted, the singer focuses his imaginative energy on his presentation. He gathers his rhetorical strength in the intensity of his singing, and the impulse to innovate comes out in the most minute embellishments that are hardly even noticeable to the casual listener but sensed on a deeper level by their effectiveness in conveying the emotional dimension of the story. This kind of epic spontaneity is present in *Mexico City Blues* most clearly in the subtle variations on the chorus form in the poem. What looks fairly restricted—a single page in a tiny notebook—becomes a source of endless variation so that no two choruses are exactly the same in form.

Clearly, however, Kerouac's poetry more closely resembles the cry of the lyric, with its emphasis on music and emotion rather than on detail and plot. Instead of a hero, the lyric poem gives us a disembodied voice, usually of unspecified race, class, or gender. Taken individually, the choruses of *Mexico City Blues* can be read as lyrics in this traditional sense. Many of them stand well on their own apart from the whole, and the structure of the poem as a whole derives some of its coherence and effect from the independent lyric qualities of the individual choruses. The independence of the choruses gives Kerouac the advantage of lyric spontaneity as well: the attempt to make a poem that follows its inspiration closely in both time and mood without the supervention of a cumbersome structure. Thus, he accesses the coherence of an overarching plan, with its attendant "small spontaneity" of embellishment, without foregoing the immediacy of lyric expression, with its "large spontaneity" of emotion controlling its form. This combination of the traditional literary extremes of spontaneity makes for balance on the deepest technical level of the poem.

The more recent source of the tradition of spontaneity in which Kerouac worked is, of course, Romantic poetry. After Wordsworth's famous definition of a poem as "the spontaneous overflow of powerful emotion," spontaneity became the bench mark of true poetry. Like the epic poets, however, even Neoclassical writers had their moments of spontaneity. Ruled by decorum, craft, and judgment, writers like Dryden, Pope, and Johnson were, nevertheless, acutely aware of the function of genius. They recognized that the well-turned phrase cannot be turned by anyone and everyone. For them, spontaneity lay in wit. It was a product of—rather than, as for the Romantics, productive of—the poetic process. In sequence, spontaneity enters near the end of composition for the Neoclassical artist and near the beginning for the Romantic artist. In most art, naturally, there is a balance between Neoclassical and Romantic spontaneity, but the choice that distinguishes these two types is one of the most profound moments of divergence in Western art. Spengler thought that it was such an important matter that he used it to characterize the transition from culture to civilization. The shift from Neoclassical to Romantic—in every culture, he believed—spelled the beginning of the end. That is, a shift in emphasis on the importance of spontaneity characterizes the culmination of a society's growth.

"Any attempt to create art," David Perkins says in his book on Wordsworth, "must cope with an intrinsic conflict between amplitude, or richness of content, and cleanliness of shape, and artists could be roughly classified by the choice they make" (44). The interesting thing about *Mexico City Blues* in this respect is that the improvisational jazz form with the repeating structure of the chorus is Kerouac's attempt to circumvent the choice. And if one thinks of it, what shape could be "cleaner" than the simplicity of open-ended repetition? In any case, while Kerouac obviously comes down on the Romantic end of the spectrum, he opts for a combination of the spontaneity of content and the spontaneity of form. This combination, like epic and lyric spontaneity, contributes to the sense of equilibrium in the poem.

In characterizing the influence of Wordsworth's attitude toward spontaneity, Perkins has this to say:

> One assumption that dominates much modern poetry is that a perception is truer, at least more fundamental and certain, than the inferences we build on it, and we must go back to primary perceptions, seizing them in their immediacy, if we have any hope of obtaining a reliable interpretation of things. (23)

Perkins argues that the Romantic valorization of spontaneity nevertheless proceeds directly from Locke's conception of the way the mind works. The Neoclassical writers emphasized the value of the inference while the Romantics emphasized the value of the perception. In this context spontaneity means sensitivity to sense perceptions and to the emotions generated by them rather than accurate recording and manipulation of the inferences drawn from the perceptions. While Kerouac does not ignore the inferences any more than the great Romantic poets did, his project is to eliminate the temporal and psychic gap between the moment of inspiration and the moment of creation. This, of course, has been the dream of Platonists for centuries. Although Kerouac recognized the existence of and need for the rational analysis that follows perception, he felt, like Wordsworth, that the sake of truth is best served by fidelity to first impressions.

As psychology developed in the nineteenth century, Locke's view of the discrete steps of mentation fell by the wayside. William James's formulation of the "stream of consciousness" took precedence. In James's view, each thought was connected in content to the one that preceded and the one that followed. The literary version of this outlook, which proceeded from impressionism, placed great value on the notation and simulation of the flow of thoughts in the characters' minds. Kerouac was enamored of the method of stream of consciousness used by James Joyce, and his poems contain a number of references to *Finnegans Wake* and other works by Joyce. Kerouac's fiction seems to be the direct descendent of Joyce's because he adapts the technique to the more personal tone of a first-person narrator. The value of spontaneity in stream of consciousness writing is to capture the transitions between past and present, present and future. The causal connections of the Lockean model of thought disappear and are replaced by an acceptance of and appreciation for the discontinuity of personality. With Joyce, the literary artist began to perceive that thought neither begins nor ends except in the most artificial and contrived senses. Unlike both the Neoclassical and Romantic modes, stream of consciousness ignores the inception and result of perception, preferring instead to focus on the process of thinking. Stream of consciousness, however, is still Romantic in its striving to appreciate the emotional significance of the moment rather than to capitalize on the rational function of the mind. While Kerouac carefully and thoughtfully adapted stream of consciousness to the postwar American scene, he did go so far as to imitate Joyce's style in a short prose work called "Old Angel Midnight," written in 1956. This story presents a parallel in his mature writing similar to his early imitation of the fiction of Thomas Wolfe and places his work squarely within the mainstream of literary tradition.

Another literary source for the tradition of spontaneity lies in Dada and Surrealism. Many of the choruses of *Mexico City Blues* have the wacky effrontery of Dadaist poetry and the dreamlike detail of Surrealism. In writers like Tzara and Breton Kerouac found precedent for yet another kind of spontaneity: an antiliterary spontaneity based on chance, accident, or arbitrariness. Already in 1952 in Mexico City, as Nicosia notes, "he had permitted accident to influence the composition of *Doctor Sax*, for example, by ending a chapter whenever Burroughs would interrupt him" (422). This use of the irrational to create form marked Kerouac's final assault on the notion of craft. By allowing the size of his notebook pages to determine the length of a chorus in his long poem, he gives up the illusion of total control. He gives in to the power of circumstance, to the determination of whim. By giving himself over to the arbitrary, the accidental, the fateful, he opens his poem to the qualities of randomness, coincidence, and inevitability that are commonly attributed to experience in life. Part of the literary heritage of spontaneity, naturally, is negative: resistance to craft, rejection of literary conventions, reluctance to depend on rational means of composition. These aspects of spontaneity, which derive from the Dadaists' and Surrealists' attack on the tradition, have the advantage, in Kerouac's poetry at least, of balancing against tradition, perhaps of preventing him from using spontaneity as a mere convention.

The contemporary manifestation of the tradition of spontaneity in American literature was the school of Confessional Poets that was developing in the 1950s during the height of Kerouac's career. The inception of John Berryman's *Dream Songs*, for instance, coincides precisely with the composition of *Mexico City Blues*. Allen Ginsberg, Kerouac's closest poet associate, was initially included among the Confessionals with Robert Lowell, Berryman, Anne Sexton, and Sylvia Plath. To my knowledge no one has ever considered Jack Kerouac a member of this school, but his passion for self-revelation, like Ginsberg's, legitimately connects him with those more mainstream poets. Here the quality of spontaneity is partly religious, partly therapeutic. It derives from the Puritan diarists, from Thoreau's injunction (in the first few pages of *Walden*) to sincerity, and from the free association techniques of 1950s Freudian therapy. All the Confessional Poets had bouts of madness, and most committed suicide. Many, like Kerouac, were at the same time deeply religious. Unlike Kerouac, however, the Confessional Poets were all thoroughly devoted to the notion of craft. In some ways then, ironically, Kerouac's affinity for open form may make him the most confessional of all. As he asked Randall Jarrell—a second generation New Critic and champion of craft in the 1950s—"How can you confess your crafty soul in craft?" (*Desolation Angels* 280). Despite this profound difference of attitude, Kerouac appears to have shared some of the goals of the most mainstream academic and intellectual group of poets of his own day, and it may be that the most distinctive difference between him and them is that his concept of spontaneity derives from a much more diverse set of sources.

In a strictly literary sense, therefore, Kerouac's use of spontaneity was reasonably flexible. M. H. Abrams, in his classic study *The Mirror and the Lamp*, noted that the great Romantic poets were not blind to "the supervention of the antithetical qualities of foresight and choice" (qtd. in Weinreich 3). This is the part of the tradition of spontaneity that allows an artistic hedge in the direction of balance, the hedge that Kerouac calls "control" in the passage from *Desolation Angels* quoted earlier. The tradition provides a counter to its own concept, a counter of which all those working in the tradition, including Kerouac, avail themselves. Nevertheless, it is obvious that Kerouac falls far on the Romantic side of the spectrum of spontaneity. John Tytell, in a chapter of *Naked Angels* called "Jack Kerouac: Eulogist of Spontaneity," argues that he expanded the tradition as he used it: "In his aesthetic of spontaneity, Kerouac extended the romantic tradition to its logical ends, far beyond the Wordsworthian idea that the writer's function was to *re*capture an action, a strongly felt emotion, in tranquility" (141). Rather, Kerouac's purpose was to use spontaneity to collapse the interval between inspiration and creation, to produce an immediate—not a mediated—version of reality to enact experience and emotions in language.

Kerouac's concept of spontaneity also has a number of other origins besides literary tradition. Conditions and events in his own life, for instance, prepared the ground for his mature acceptance of the spontaneous in his writing. Prevailing attitudes toward psychology were also important formative influences. And there were related concepts in the other arts that provided Kerouac with an appreciation of spontaneity by analogy. In dealing with these extraliterary origins, I want first to trace the development of spontaneity to its biographical sources to give some sense of how Kerouac's unique experience led him to modify this rather ambiguous literary technique.

Many commentators have discussed Kerouac's linguistic roots in the spoken French of his hometown. Some, like Tom Clark, even believe that Kerouac's bilingualism is the single most important fact of his life. What I find significant about this argument is that Kerouac's French-Canadian heritage is almost synonymous with spoken language. It's as though his writing life were an equation that attempted to resolve orality and literacy—French standing for the oral and English for the literate.

Kerouac's class origin reinforced his ethnic heritage in this respect. Again, as the passage from *Desolation Angels* at the head of this chapter demonstrates, his notion of spontaneity is somehow tied to the oral storytelling of lower-middle class life. Lowell French-Canadians, unlike the local Greeks or Irish, were notoriously antiliterate. Kerouac preserved his native orality throughout his life by speaking French with his mother at home. There was never a time, I imagine, at which he lost his awareness of the very different character of spontaneity in speech as opposed to writing. This oral spontaneity was further conditioned by the social nature of the French-Canadian community. Kerouac's oral language was bound to memories of home, family, and social life; it was the language of interaction with the familiar world of childhood. Because of the primarily conversational nature of his first language, Kerouac knew intimately the kind of spontaneity required of an oral poet. As he learned English, he also learned a new kind of spontaneity, one that was accessible in private through writing.

From adolescence he had a foot in both worlds, and he intuitively applied his sense of oral spontaneity to writing. This too has the tinge of Romanticism about it, following Wordsworth's imperative that poetry use the language of common men (Tytell 147). The conversational tone of Kerouac's prose and poetry is only the most obvious support for such a supposition.

Later, after his time at Columbia during the war, Kerouac encountered the very embodiment of spontaneity. This personification was, of course, Neal Cassady. "For Kerouac and Ginsberg," Gifford and Lee point out, "Neal provided an example of instinct in action" (87). But even more than his headlong pursuit of experience and his notorious skill behind the wheel, Cassady's own writing provided Kerouac with a model of spontaneous technique. "The discovery of a style of my own based on spontaneous get-with-it," he once said, "came after reading the marvelous free-narrative letters of Neal Cassady, a great writer who happens also to be the Dean Moriarty of *On the Road*" (qtd. in Gifford and Lee 87). Cassady announced, in fact, at the end of the "Great Sex Letter" (in which he recounted a cross-country bus ride, including the seduction of a young high school teacher in Kansas City) that he had been trying to produce "a continuous chain of undisciplined thought" (Nicosia 183).

As Kerouac and Cassady began to trade bits of writerly advice, they simultaneously honed their concept of spontaneity. One of Kerouac's first admonitions to his buddy was to "write with the zeal of a benny addict" (Gifford and Lee 107). Cassady responded rather cautiously: "To play safe force yourself to think and then write rather than think what to write about and what to say as you write" (Nicosia 186).

Not long after his first meeting with Cassady in the winter of 1946, Kerouac turned his attention to his friend as an object as well as a subject. Cassady provided the model for the characters of Paul Hathaway in *The Town and the City*, the remarkable Dean Moriarty in *On the Road*, and Cody Pomeray in *Visions of Cody*. By the early 1950s, several years before the composition of *Mexico City Blues*, as Charters says, "writing about his visions of Neal had loosened Kerouac and brought him, through his sketching method of free association, to confront his own memories about his own life without fear or evasion" (148). Nicosia quotes another letter from Cassady to Kerouac that sums up the feeling of absolute originality that could only be achieved by employing the spontaneous method: "One should write, as nearly as possible, as if one were the first person on earth and was humbly and sincerely putting on paper that which he saw and experienced, loved and lost" (203).

Consequently, by the time Kerouac wrote *Mexico City Blues* in the summer of 1955, he had already been discussing his theory of spontaneity with friends and practicing it in his prose for the better part of a decade. After having fallen out with Cassady over the issue of Edgar Cayce, Kerouac found a willing ear in another longtime correspondent, Allen Ginsberg, and simultaneously provided a great service to American literature. As Kerouac was traveling to Mexico that summer, Ginsberg had begun to write "Howl," which is, along with *Mexico City Blues*, the great monument to spontaneous composition in Postmodern American poetry. "It was to teach Ginsberg about spontaneous poetry," Nicosia says, "that Kerouac sat down with coffee and a joint on his tiny rooftop for a few hours every morning, pencilling little blues poems in his notebooks" (480). Clark, in fact, perceives the influence, calling "Howl" a "work that reflected [Ginsberg's] serious study not only of Kerouac's spontaneous writing mode but also of 'the myth of Lester Young' as described by Kerouac" (139). Several years later, Ginsberg repaid Kerouac for his tuition by coining a phrase to describe the compositional method they both shared: "spontaneous bop prosody" (Clark 173). In any case, as an influence on "Howl" and as a poem in its own right, *Mexico City Blues* is the epitome of perfection in Kerouac's spontaneous method. It incorporates all his modifications of the theory into a remarkably free, yet carefully controlled, work of art. In discussing Robert Creeley's response to the poem, Nicosia says that Kerouac's friend and fellow poet saw his "'ability to translate immediate sensation into immediately actual language'" (521). In this instance, at least, the method succeeded miraculously well.

As is typical of Kerouac, less than a year later the spontaneous method had run to excess. In a little cabin he shared with Gary Snyder in Mill Valley, California, Kerouac experienced one of those antithetical moments that color the lives of artists. Within days of each other, he composed his tribute to absolute spontaneity, *Old Angel Midnight*, a retelling of the creation story in the mode of *Finnegans Wake*, and the avowedly antispontaneous American sutra, *The Scripture of the Golden Eternity*. This latter, composed at the suggestion of Gary Snyder, was done in pencil so that it could be easily revised to preserve, clarify, and convey its Buddhist content. Yet it was written in a single sitting in the course of one night.

Kerouac considered *Old Angel Midnight* to have been produced by a kind of automatic writing, "not like Yeats's wife, that in a trance he wrote words inspired by some commanding spirit, but simply that he wrote—and by his own admission this was the only instance of his doing so—without the slightest effort to censor or alter his expression" (Nicosia 517). Although it ostensibly follows the method of stream of consciousness writing, *Old Angel Midnight* bears some resemblance to the poem that concludes *Big Sur*, which imitates the sounds of the Pacific. That is, the attempt to capture the nuanced transitions from thought to thought combines with the attempt to record the impressions of perception as they are being received. "In 'Old Angel Midnight,'" McNally says, "Kerouac tried to catch the sound of all tongues, the infinite sound of the universe as it floated into his window late at night, and for the first time he permitted himself the absolute freedom to write anything that came into his head" (216). This exercise in free writing has never been published in a trade edition, so it remains to be seen how successful it is in terms of readability, but in terms of the theory of spontaneous composition, it marks the furthest extreme of experiment in Kerouac's career. After 1956, he returned to a spontaneously modified autobiographical realism.

Besides these specifics of Kerouac's life, there was much in the general cultural milieu of America in the 1950s and in the lifestyle he chose to lead that recommended spontaneity not only as an artistic method but as the most effective response to day-to-day living. On the most obvious level, spontaneity represented a reaction against the rigid social mores of the developing suburban culture. Yet on another level, Kerouac's compositional method simply imitated—or perhaps parodied—the culture in which it developed. The torrent of words loosed by the spontaneous method effectively mimics 1950s overproduction. To make the product easily available, you must produce more of it than is actually needed. A good deal of waste results.

Then there was, as Aldous Huxley pointed out, that unique characteristic of the modern world: speed. Everything about *On the Road* betokens speed; it might almost be considered the primary content of the novel. But more importantly, speed was essential to Kerouac's spontaneous method. Mindful of Shelley's metaphor of the imagination as dying ember, Kerouac strove to catch up with his own inspiration. In doing so, he embodied the essence of his era.

Kerouac's bohemian lifestyle—itself redolent of spontaneity in its uninterrupted flow of experience, its obsessive extemporaneous talk, and its improvisational jazz soundtrack—was an attempt to avoid the restrictions of society without depriving himself of its pleasures. Drugs—especially alcohol—intensified the chaos of loose living and created a kind of artificial spontaneity by partially removing the controls of will and conscience. Freedom, too, was the goal proposed by the dominant philosophy of the day, existentialism. The teachings of Sartre and Camus demanded the deepest and most honest relations with other human beings at every moment. This kind of living, whatever its flaws, requires supple and resilient reflexes. It is not—despite all the bourgeois criticism—an easy life, either materially or emotionally. Spontaneity, as the large number of bohemian suicides demonstrates, can be exhausting.

Another main feature of the intellectual life of the postwar period was the growth in popularity of depth psychology, especially Freudianism. Though Kerouac was never professionally psychoanalyzed, several of his friends, including Ginsberg, were. Moreover, Kerouac did allow William S. Burroughs to practice the techniques of Freudian analysis on him. He also had contact with Navy psychiatrists who facilitated his discharge from the service. The Surrealist preoccupation with dreams played into his concern about the structure of the mind, and even drunkenness provided a wealth of data to contend with. Out of the general preoccupation with madness that characterizes modern European civilization (as Foucault has shown in *Madness and Modern Civili-*

zation), Kerouac chose the therapeutic technique of free associa-
tion as one of the models for his theory of spontaneity. Only if
the conscious mind were allowed free rein—that is, only if will
and intellect were somehow neutralized, and instinct were allowed
to express itself—could the subconscious and unconscious con-
tents rise to the surface. *Mexico City Blues* is, among other things,
an exercise in self-analysis. Its improvisational content, repeating
form, and arbitrary limitations create an environment similar to
the psychiatrist's office. The desired effect is to unleash the power
of the id, and it is no wonder that here, as elsewhere in Kerouac's
writing, he uses the word *mad* with such casual force.

Kerouac made every effort to access his intuition, to remove
the censor, even to the extent of allowing his mistakes to stand
uncorrected and unrevised. He understood the value of these in
the Freudian sense, as keys to some meaning that could not be ex-
pressed appropriately in its own terms. He also uses his own
dreams and those of Garver to underscore the importance of the
symbolic imagery of life and of poetry. Occasionally, he evinces a
clearly Reichian view of his own activity, understanding writing as
a form of sexual expression and believing that "the more feeling it
released (like Reich's postulated electrical discharge during or-
gasm), the more satisfactory the experience for both writer and
reader" (Nicosia 446). But always he sensed the connection of
psychology to literary tradition. Kerouac knew, as Nicosia ob-
serves, that "writing by free association had been done extensively
by Proust, as well as many of the Romantic poets, including
Wordsworth and Coleridge, and its roots went back to the lyrical
poets of Greece and Rome" (186). In this, as in many other areas,
Kerouac made the intuitive mixture of the literary and the extra-
literary that kept his writing both topical and universal.

Analogies to spontaneity in other arts also help ensure the
universality of Kerouac's writing. In fact, though he actually be-
gan to practice spontaneous writing with the composition of the
scroll mansucript of *On the Road* in April 1951—before he even
had a name for his method—the theory seems to have developed
out of a suggestion made to Kerouac by his artist friend Ed White
in October 1951. The sketching that White proposed "was at first
strictly an on-the-spot technique, but it quickly developed into a

rapid notational method for transcribing from memory and imagination as well" (Clark 102). Gifford and Lee quote Burroughs—whose cut-up method of composition, while very different from Kerouac's spontaneity, springs from similar sources and aims at similar effects—as saying that Kerouac always preferred the first version of what he wrote. Burroughs characterizes Kerouac's theory as one "of sketching with words, and of the flow and using the first version—the first words that came" (190). The effect of the method on Kerouac's writing was profound, as Nicosia says, "for it permitted him to make the process of writing into the subject of his writing" (359). Like the action painters in the abstract expressionist movement (e.g., Jackson Pollack), Kerouac created a method of composition that kept him fully aware that he was describing the method itself as he used it to describe characters, actions, and scenes.

Music, of course, is the other art that influenced Kerouac's concept of spontaneity. Nicosia finds a personal motivation for Kerouac's application of the technique of jazz improvisation to his method of writing:

> Weary of writing in solitude, Kerouac loved projects in which everyone could participate, and he especially liked to see people pooling their talents just as jazz musicians in a band stimulated one another. Spontaneity increased when one person's impulses bounced freely off another's; hence music served as a chief metaphor for the type of creativity he sought. (293)

From his days at Horace Mann Prep School in the late 1930s, when he began to develop his taste for jazz, Kerouac expressed his affinity for the method of improvisation (Clark 41). Twenty years later, when he had mastered the literary version of the technique, he had a chance to practice it by improvising the narration for a movie made by Robert Frank and Alfred Leslie called *Pull My Daisy*. Kerouac had already written a play that incorporated the plot of the film. Nevertheless, in two takes he made his spontaneous commentary. David Amram, the musician who provided the score for the film, described Kerouac's effort as that of "a great jazzman . . . he played around the chords or played around the situation, improvising on certain things, and made a beautiful tapestry out of nothing" (qtd. in Clark 176).

In addition to the other arts, religion provided Kerouac with analogies to his spontaneous method of writing. Catholic confession as well as Buddhism gave Kerouac precedents for spontaneity. He found that not only did the buddhas and bodhisattvas he admired discover enlightenment through intuitive processes, but also that the sutras explicitly advised readers "to answer questions spontaneously with no recourse to discriminating thinking" (Goddard 102, 112). Finally, Nicosia says, "Kerouac's Buddhist studies confirmed that spontaneity was the only teacher of higher laws" (479). In fact, Kerouac apparently used his sketching technique to write *Some of the Dharma*, his notes and summaries of his Buddhist readings (Gifford and Lee 186).

As fame and alcoholism began to increase Kerouac's tendency toward megalomania in the 1960s, he started to think of his writing in terms of classic Christian spontaneity—the automatic writing of scripture. In a 1960 reference to *Book of Dreams*, Kerouac claimed that "he was a channel of God, his writing a scripture" (McNally 292). Just the year before he had told a friend that "when God speaks" you "just take it down" (Nicosia 595). Several years later, in a radio interview in his hometown, Kerouac told listeners in Lowell: "Once God moves the hand, you go back and revise, it's a sin!" (Nicosia 638) The radical freedom of the stream of conscious style of *Old Angel Midnight* eventually became the hoarse cry of the neglected prophet.

Determining the sum of Kerouac's attitudes toward spontaneity and describing how these attitudes make a theory and practice of composition is somewhat difficult. At least one of Kerouac's Columbia friends, Hal Chase, observed that Kerouac was himself "virtually incapable of spontaneous behavior" (Nicosia 165). It seems to Nicosia that "Kerouac was learning to improvise his life much as he had learned to improvise literature" (196), so that his theory of spontaneity may have been a reaction to the deep-seated sense of propriety or decorum that thwarted his childhood freedom. He used his art, then, as a model for his life. By freeing his writing, he attempted to free himself. Because he wanted to reach down deep within himself "to tap the preliterate sources of art" (McNally 168), he was forced to abandon conventional methods and styles. This abandonment also represented his response to postwar America: "After attempting to write 'careful "Johnsonian" sentences' he realized that classical English prose 'just doesn't EXPRESS the swirl of things as they are in this swirling age'" (Nicosia 659).

Kerouac's phenomenal memory may have created an illusion of spontaneity to some degree as well. The diction and tone of great passages in Shakespeare Kerouac had memorized often came out in his writing, for instance (Nicosia 500). His memory also enabled him to compose in his head "so that the actual putting of words on paper was but a mechanical extension of the process" (Nicosia 521). His friend and fellow novelist John Clellon Holmes has described the composition of the scroll version of *On the Road* as a kind of transcription: "He just flung it down. He could disassociate himself from his fingers, and he was simply following the movie in his head" (qtd. in Gifford and Lee 156). Malcolm Cowley, who edited *On the Road*, used the metaphor of toothpaste coming from a tube to describe Kerouac's attitude toward spontaneous composition (Gifford and Lee 206), and Kerouac himself, explaining the technique to a friend in Lowell, likened it to turning on a faucet to wait for the water to turn cold (Nicosia 600). Yet Kerouac was "no fanatic about spontaneity," Nicosia asserts, and he "understood that certain types of writing require revision" (480). Holmes has, in fact, observed that "typing to Kerouac—in Kerouac's career—meant rewriting" (Gifford and Lee 157). And Regina Weinreich has expressed the opinion that, in a broader sense, in retelling his own story in the course of the Duluoz Legend, "repetition in fact becomes Kerouac's control" (5).

So Kerouac's spontaneous method was far from absolute, and while he clearly valorized the immediate, unpremeditated response in writing, he did not write out of thin air. He wrote from memory and in response to the stimulation of his senses. He may have, following Neal Cassady's notion of "prevision," revised in his head before he wrote. This is hardly an innovation in poetics. Still, Kerouac did possess the magical gift of spontaneity (Gifford and Lee 211). John Tytell sums up his method best:

Kerouac knew that the integrity of pure experience and the feelings that actually attended the moment of occurrence could best be achieved when the writer removed all procedural lags, when his momentum was such as to obviate the Flaubertian obsession with the precise word. (144)

There is a sense in which all creation—all thought, indeed—involves complete disjunction. The true work of art must break with the past, with convention, with the habitual, with the anticipated. All imagination, in this sense, is spontaneous. But this disjunction may seem mystical, even frightening (as it betokens loss of control) to the nonartist. Better, I think, to conceive of Kerouac's spontaneity as a procedure or technique (which can be practiced, learned, and perfected) for maintaining constant awareness. His "spontaneous bop prosody" represents, therefore, a metaphor for consciousness. His desire for egolessness must have led him to conclude that the ego is only the illusion of continuity: the "I" that was yesterday is the "I" that will be tomorrow. But in spontaneous method, only the "I" at the moment of writing exists, and though that "I" is written, it sounds like a spoken "I": momentary, voluntary, persistent but not persisting. As Tytell notes, "Kerouac's insights were the releases of a man who knew words so well that he did not have to pause to shape the flow" (209).

The fundamental difficulty in applying the concept of spontaneity to aesthetics is that, unlike other mental processes such as memory, it cannot be accurately measured. In this respect it resembles intention, and in fact, spontaneity seems to be one aspect of artistic intention. Did Kerouac intend for *Mexico City Blues* to be written spontaneously? Clearly he did, but how do we know he was always true to his intention? What, in other words, are the objective signs of spontaneity in the poem? And how can merely conventional spontaneity be distinguished from intentional spontaneity? To trace the effects of spontaneity in *Mexico City Blues*, I will first recall the setting in which Kerouac wrote the poem; then I will point out some of the conventional devices he uses to create the impression of spontaneity; and finally, I will examine the form to discover firmer evidence of the effects of true spontaneity.

The circumstances of the composition of *Mexico City Blues* in Mexico City in the summer of 1955 exhibit many of the characteristics associated with traditional literary spontaneity, especially the kind commonly found in Dadaism. First, Kerouac commonly wrote choruses under the influence of marijuana. It was his common practice to write under the influence of drugs, usually benzedrine. Novels such as *On the Road* and *The Subterraneans* show sure signs of the effects of speed in method of composition, form, and content. The same is true of *Mexico City Blues*. Much of the word play, disjunction of themes, and lack of transitions is characteristic of stoned conversations. These same characteristics are also hallmarks of spontaneity.

Another practice Kerouac followed in composing the poem was to limit the size of each chorus to the length of a small notebook page. This required that the closure of each chorus be more or less arbitrary (i.e., spontaneous). Third, he wrote in response to an interlocutor. Despite that Kerouac often memorized actual conversations in order to transfer them into his novels, the collaboration he engaged in with Garver during the writing of *Mexico City Blues* is unique in his writing. More than the conversational tone of his novels, this poem actually became a conversation of sorts, and that is partly what lends it its distinctly oral character. These restrictions are no more arbitrary than the formalities of craft, except that their effect is presumably unpredictable.

Many of the choruses Kerouac devoted directly to Bill Garver have the quality of found poems, like the long quotations in the "33rd" and "34th" choruses, for instance, in which Garver delivers a statement of his own spontaneous philosophy of living. Others, like the "72nd" and "73rd" choruses, merely weave in brief excerpts of conversation to give them the same kind of presence as a live recording. Still others, like the "139th Chorus," reconstitute one of Garver's stories or sayings in the context of Buddhism or one of the other themes of the poem. The total effect of all the Garver choruses is to give the reader a sense of eavesdropping. The ongoing conversation between the singer and Garver brings down the fourth wall and makes the poem a stage.

The conversational tone also inclines the reader to be more of a participant than an observer. While *Mexico City Blues* consistently retains its dramatic quality, it also attempts to break down the distinction between performer and audience, a technique traditionally used in avant-garde theater to elicit spontaneous response from both actors and spectators.

Without doubting Kerouac's fidelity to the spontaneous method, I should note that several of the choruses do employ rhetorical conventions of spontaneity. These may either flow from the method itself, or they may be unconsciously assimilated devices that Kerouac used to communicate or heighten the effect of spontaneity in the poem. Some of these involve real or simulated lapses of memory. In an earlier chapter I discussed the "38th Chorus," in which the resolution of the statement is suspended while the singer tries, out loud, to recall the name of the Roman sea god. This is precisely the kind of matter that would be excised by a writer with a Neoclassical method. By not only letting it stand but actually calling attention to it, Kerouac attempts to give an object lesson in his method. He uses the same device—although it is open to question whether it is a device or a pure expression of sentiment—in the "53rd Chorus," where the singer asks "what the hell's the name / of that instrument / the Aeolian Lyre." This passage is interesting because the Aeolian harp was a favorite image of the Romantic poets for describing the way in which the imagination responds spontaneously to nature. Kerouac playfully combines his version of spontaneity with the older one through a conversational device so simple it can easily be overlooked. These choruses also appear to adopt the Freudian attitude that mistakes in the act of composition may very well be more revealing than successful articulation.

A number of narrative intrusions perform similar functions in the poem. The "38th Chorus," for example, begins "(Pome beginning with parenthesis:— / God!)," as though the singer were shocked by his own spontaneity. The "60th Chorus" likewise combines narrative intrusion with the dream device of Surrealism. The first stanza begins: "C i l / Rubberbands Seventyfivedollars / I came out of the dream." The illusion (at least) here is that the singer is transcribing the tail end of his dream, which merges with the composition of the chorus. Late in the poem, another such intrusion provides an unusual closure to a chorus, the "209th." The last four lines not only cancel what has gone before in the chorus, but also heavily underscore the final couplet, which appears to be the result of this spontaneous revision of the topic:

> I got the woozes
> Said the wrong thing
> Want gold want gold
> Gold of eternity.

In the "216th-A Chorus," one of several that announce the approaching conclusion of the poem, the intrusion sounds particularly ironic in terms of the theme of spontaneity: "Fuck," the singer intones, "I'm tired of this imagery." The effect of this, which is much like Kerouac's fictional technique, is to create a separate level of spontaneity through which the singer can interrupt himself to achieve a more honest utterance.

Much of the word play in *Mexico City Blues*, especially when it approaches nonsense, also contributes to the impression of spontaneity. Of course, like glossolalia in religion, nonsense does create spontaneity of meaning. Words joined more with regard for sound have a remarkable capacity for developing sense. Again, the "38th Chorus" contains an appropriate example: "Marc / Brandelian Antonio / Julius Marc McAnthony" comments on the image of Cleopatra's knot more efficiently than might otherwise be possible. There are many other examples of this conventional use of nonsense in the poem, ranging from "Pull My Daisy"-style doggerel to attempts to render street sounds in language to this intriguing imitation of typing errors in the "142nd Chorus":

> Truss in dental
> Pop Oly Ruby
> Tobby Tun w d l
> l x t s 8 7 r e r (.

The overall effect of such usages is to create the sense of play for the reader. Because the singer gives no serious forethought to the construction of the words—or so it seems—whatever meaning or lack of meaning results can only be the product of accident: pure spontaneity. In the "236th Chorus" he even appears to be answering a knock at his door, inviting the visitor (perhaps his readers) to join him in the composition of the poem.

Beyond these various conventions—and it is open to question whether they are products of or productive of spontaneity—Kerouac also treats spontaneity explicitly as one of the minor themes in the poem. He rejects the radio because it purveys the "automatic / Words of others" ("119th Chorus), and like Whitman, he admires animals for their spontaneity ("206th Chorus"). He plays with the "dominos of chance" ("232nd Chorus") and admits "crashing interruptions" ("171st Chorus") into his composition. He even advises his readers to try to apply his method of composition to the act of reading the poem: "The thing is to express / the very substance of your thoughts / as you read this" ("67th Chorus"). Then near the end of the poem, he seems to lose patience with his readers/listeners. "O come off it," he exclaims, "the vast canopial / Assemblies wait for yr honest spontaneous reply" ("218th Chorus"). Here I sense the singer is genuinely inviting his audience to participate in the spontaneous act of creation by transforming the act of reading into a true dialogue with another consciousness.

When the singer announces in the "5th Chorus" that "Samuel Johnson / Is Under the sea," he may very well be announcing an attack on craft in the poem. He speaks nostalgically of the "original mind of babyhood" ("17th Chorus") and ties the whole issue of spontaneity carefully to his Buddhist studies. In the "28th Chorus" the singer explains in detail how the "Craft Gleam" follows from the act of discrimination in the mind. Discrimination itself, in the Buddhist way of thinking, is already a step away from the recognition of the unchanging essence of reality, which is emptiness. Craft, in terms of the search for enlightenment, is an act of supererogation. It also runs counter to an acceptance of the flow of events that Kerouac, in his Taoist leanings, considered to be the fundamental principle of existence. In "real life not / still life" ("152nd Chorus"), he believed, "Everything is in the same moment" ("121st Chorus"). Craft, therefore, falsifies the flux, makes it appear stable. Further, by his Buddhist lights Kerouac believed that the changing course of events was itself an illusion. That is, the Taoist view is the most realistic view of the way things are, but because it discriminates events and objects, it is still deluded. At the core, Kerouac believed, lies the changeless essence of emptiness. Consequently, craft seemed to him not only unrealistic on the face of it, but ultimately counterproductive. It fails to account for the fact that "everything is in the same moment" and that, paradoxically, "it aint happenin now" ("158th Chorus").

Kerouac's desire, expressed in *Mexico City Blues*, is to become a "Convulsive writer of Poems" in the Absurdist lineage of Pirandello. That is why he submerges Johnson, and it may be why he thinks of

> hell's clutters
> that meated dante
> when he virgilized
> his poign.   ("186th Chorus")

He is certainly thrilled by the possibility of escaping the influence of craft embodied by the great masters. Perhaps recalling the transcriptions in *Visions of Cody*, the singer extols "tape, a new kind of voice, / sung for the self" ("172nd Chorus"), as though the very presence of an audience had placed too severe a restriction on originality. The singer's willingness to "stop & jump to other field" ("33rd Chorus") or to accept the "sudden thought of India" ("165th Chorus") in the midst of composition leads him to the culmination of spontaneous poetry—"The orgasm / Of the moon / And the June" ("83rd Chorus").

The "195th Chorus" marks the climax of the theme of spontaneity in the poem: "The songs that erupt / Are gist of the poesy." Its tone shifts from a reverence for the "ragged" human beauty revealed by the spontaneous method to a wistful comparison with the music of the spheres. Finally, the last stanza begins ambiguously with a critique of "human poetries / With God as their design." Since Kerouac, even as he studied Buddhism, was a theist, it is difficult to know whether he is including his own spontaneous poem in this category or contrasting it with traditional religious poems. The content of the second stanza, with its paradoxical description of the stars as both moving and motionless, real and unreal, suggests the latter. Practically speaking, it doesn't matter, since the chorus ends not with an attempt at intellectual resolution, but with a spontaneous outburst, an exuberant request for music.

One of the many small beauties of *Mexico City Blues* is the way the theme of spontaneity becomes embodied in form. Examples of this embodiment can be found in individual choruses and in the structure of the poem as a whole. For instance, the shift in tone in the "195th Chorus" represents a paradigm for the dramatization of spontaneity. In twenty-one short lines it moves from seriousness to slapstick. This same sort of shift, in both tone and content, can be found in many other choruses. The "145th Chorus," for example, begins with a surrealist account of someone shooting up morphine with a needle the size of the Empire State Building. This becomes a metaphor for the 1950s obsession with communism, but the last stanza, instead of extending the metaphor or clarifying the meaning, simply lists the names of four figures in American literary history. The disjunction between beginning and end enacts the discontinuity of thought that represents one aspect of spontaneity. This is not to say that all the choruses follow this pattern, but a third to a half show similar disjunctions, and the choruses that display more coherence provide a contrast that, in many cases, makes the others even more startling.

A middle ground between the spontaneous quality of the parts and the spontaneous quality of the whole exists in a set of truncated choruses that serve the musical function of rests. In conversational terms they resemble the pauses that accommodate the generation of speech. In Buddhist terms they allow us to hear the silence that subtends sound. Nicosia calls the first of these, the "11th Chorus," a "paradigm of Kerouac's technique" (481). In it, five disjointed lines are followed by a large space, which is followed by a parenthesis: "(musician stops, / brooding on bandstand)." Nicosia sees this as a comment on the poem's "failure to get started" (481), but *Mexico City Blues* begins with such self-assurance that it seems likely that this chorus has a more extensive significance. It alludes to Stendhal and to drugs. The combination of the two leads to silence. The musician has not failed to begin, he is brooding, literally hatching a new idea about writing using narcotics as a metaphor for spontaneity.

The "36th Chorus" also connects drugs and writing, under the heading of contemplation. "No direction to go," the singer realizes, "(but) / (in)ward." Then he muses, "Hm," and concludes: "(ripping of paper indicates / helplessness anyway)." Perhaps we are supposed to imagine that Kerouac has torn the notebook page on which he is composing the chorus and to wonder whether this happens accidentally or on purpose. Astute commentator that he is, Nicosia has also noticed this, and he determines that the ripping is purposeful: "a literal account of the poet's frustration" (482). Again, I think it is more symbolic of spontaneity. What the singer finds within himself is the utter arbitrariness of continuity, so that whatever happens, including the ripping of the notebook paper, has significance for him. This is the opposite of frustration, as the bemused tone of the closure indicates.

Likewise, the "138th Chorus" begins with an assertion of the eternal fellaheen culture. Kerouac envisions himself living as an Indian in Culiacan, one of the opium producing areas of Mexico. But this vision is succeeded by another long blank, then the parenthetical comment: "(BLANK, the singer / sings nothing)." This too is much more than a lapse because one of the results of Kerouac's Buddhist study is the realization that, as he says in the "118th Chorus," "I've had times of no-singing, / they were the same." In *Mexico City Blues*, I believe, the silence and the sound are to be construed as one. The "songs that erupt" can only erupt from silence, and their very "eruption"—their spontaneous coming-into-being—proves that in substance they are identical with silence. These three choruses—the "11th," "36th," and "138th"— emphasize the connection between the religious and artistic functions of spontaneity by using drugs as a metaphoric catalyst. Spontaneous composition, for Kerouac, requires that thinking be stopped, and this

> which modern
> Society has branded "Loafing," is
> made available to people now
> apparently only by junk.   ("6th Chorus")

The artificial means of spontaneity is preferred by industrialized societies because it accords with the speed of technology in other areas of life. Kerouac, as both religious seeker and artist, was quick to pick up on the symbolic as well as the practical value of drugs, and he preserved his moral neutrality by being able to draw a clear analogy between the spontaneity facilitated by drugs, the spontaneity that betokens enlightenment, and the spontaneity that he made the goal of his artistic endeavor.

The improvisational jazz form of *Mexico City Blues*, unlike the narrative forms of most long poems, allows for great flexibility in the structure of individual choruses and complete discretion about the introduction of themes. In this respect the poem, as Kerouac apparently recognized even as he wrote (see the "44th," "75th," and "207th" choruses), more closely resembles Pound's *Cantos* than any other long modernist poem. The singer digresses and reintroduces themes at will, and the near-chaos that results from this spontaneity becomes, for the Postmodern reader, one of the prime attractions of the form. The transitions between the more unified sections of *Mexico City Blues* begin to show readers what Kerouac means by spontaneous writing.

In the Lowell Cantò, for example, the "87th" through "104th" choruses are preceded by a discussion of suicide that begins in the "79th Chorus." This prelude incorporates dialogue from Garver and the words of "Harvest Moon," giving it a truly surreal quality. How does this prepare the reader for the second longest sequence of related choruses in the poem? Though there are connections to be made between suicide and growing up and between romance and family life, it is probably not a preparation at all in the traditional sense of craft. Rather, the transition simply happens, as it must have happened in Kerouac's mind during the composition of the poem, more or less arbitrarily. He preserves this arbitrariness and leaves his readers to puzzle out its significance, if indeed it has any.

The same may be said of the transition that follows the Lowell Canto. The "105th Chorus" launches into a full-blown discussion of essence as emptiness. This discussion, counterpoised against the autobiographical material that precedes it, functions metaphorically, as two elements are joined to create new meanings by forcing a comparison. Again, the connection between childhood and essence is not entirely lacking in logic, but the way in which the singer presents the new topic emphasizes the disjunction more than the continuity. Similarly the Essence of Existence Canto, which extends from the "182nd Chorus" to the "205th Chorus," is introduced by a chorus about whores and pimps. The transition away from this section, the longest chain of choruses in the poem, is not nearly so abrupt, but it does leave much to the imagination.

From the perspective of the long Modernist poem, this lack of transitions may look like a development of technique, a new function of a revised tradition. From inside the poem, however, the abrupt shift of topics, tones, and forms emphasizes the importance of the theory of spontaneity. The reader—even a reader familiar with *The Waste Land* and *The Cantos*—is drawn into the net. He or she must begin to ponder the issue of spontaneity, to wonder how it can be ascertained or even recognized in a work of art, and finally to imagine how it can be applied to the art of reading as well as the art of writing. Ultimately—and this may have been one of Kerouac's reasons for relying so heavily on the theory—there is no way to prove objectively the presence of spontaneity in a text. Spontaneity is only subjectively verifiable. Only the doer knows whether the deed was done without planning, premeditation, or ulterior motives. Objectively, a reader can only form an impression. For me, however, it is enough that Kerouac believed he was being spontaneous when he wrote. The value this places on spontaneity is partly responsible for shifting his poetry away from Modernist technique toward a spiritually renewed poetics. Of all the potential rewards of spontaneity—both in Kerouac's writing and in life—the most important is the conviction it gives a person that originality is possible, that with constant awareness each passing moment becomes rich beyond measure, and that, far from signaling loss of control, spontaneity is perhaps the most meaningful way of asserting one's complete volition.

8

Finding the Form

Reverent awe before that which is independent of one's self, things ordained and fixed by law, the alien powers of the world, is the source from which the elementary formative acts, one and all, spring.

In *Big Sur*, Kerouac's most pessimistic novel, Duluoz (the Kerouac character and narrator) recounts a pleasant morning conversation with the experimental poet Pat McLear (modeled on Michael McClure):

"Do you know that when I read your poems Mexico City Blues," McLear says, "I immediately turned around and started writing a brand new way, you enlightened me with that book."

Duluoz replies: "But it's nothing like what you do, in fact it's miles away, I am a language spinner and you're an idea man" (123).

From the very beginning of literature, poets have divided their attention between the effort to write long, comprehensive poems that reflect the intuitions of a unified sensibility and short, analytic poems that express a unique response to a single moment in time. After the Romantic period, however, the desire to condense the epic or to expand the lyric has caused the two basic modes of poetic apprehension to grow closer together. In America, Whitman's *Song of Myself* and the tightly knit series of Emily Dickinson's poems represent the pressure towards the middle from either side. Of course, there had been precedent, even in the ancient forms. Love poetry, especially since the stirrings of the Renaissance, has tended toward a set of lyrics unified by the presence of the beloved in each poem. From the songs of the troubadours, later poets developed the sonnet sequence, which reached its zenith in the work of Shakespeare, whose lyrics are rich in narrative and philosophical possibilities. It is no accident that Elizabeth Barrett Browning returned to the sonnet sequence as the most appropriate means of uttering an extended cry of the heart. In this century, poets such as W. H. Auden and Edna St. Vincent Millay have attempted to fuse lyric and narrative modes in the sonnet sequence. Kerouac, too, shows his inclination toward this form in his "limping sonnet," the "20th Chorus," and again, ironically, in the "63rd Chorus."

Christopher Smart, who was much admired by Allen Ginsberg, had earlier devised an alternative means—spurred by madness—of extending the lyric moment into a long poem. Smart's was a kind of cumulative method, composing one line a day to create a long poem whose narrative is characterized by its very disconnectedness. It was precisely this method Kerouac used to fashion one of the densest choruses of *Mexico City Blues*, the "230th Chorus." Modern poets, including Eliot with his raft of quotations, have preferred Smart's way without, however, abandoning the method of repetition in the long sequence poem. Kerouac manages to combine the methods, and it is worth noting the tension between the cumulative approach—embodied for Kerouac in the metaphor of improvisation—and the sequence approach—represented by the strict limitation on the length of the chorus. The forward march of accumulation and the regressive character of repetition strike a balance that both preserves the integrity of individual choruses and promotes unity in the poem as a whole.

The present century has witnessed a continuation of the search for new ways to combine the long and short poem. Edgar Lee Masters, for instance, spun out a series of short soliloquies unified by the speakers' citizenship in Spoon River. And Eliot, who preferred the long poem as his means of expression, never-theless chose the metaphor of the musical quartet for the organization of his greatest work—not a little song (*sonetto*) but chamber music. Yet the structure provides for a unity in its divisions and allows for repetition.

Eliot's model in this, as in his earlier work, may have been his mentor, Pound. *The Cantos* are, in fact, the supreme expression of the attempt to combine epic and lyric in the Modern period. The canto itself, another version of the "song," is internally independent in form yet indefinitely repeatable. Hart Crane, though he chose to organize his long poem around an image, nevertheless recognized the need for some musical structure within *The Bridge*. Some poets who developed and deviated from the Modern tradition have continued to adapt musical form to poetry. Louis Zukovsky, for instance, has provided a musical score as one of four levels of meaning in his long poem *Z*. I imagine that in Zukovsky's case, as in Kerouac's, musical form signifies some attempt to separate form from content, not in a Neoclassical fashion, but in a way that both extends and breaks from the Modernist insistence on the discovery of new forms for each expression.

On the other side, William Butler Yeats provides the best example of the Modernist poet who chose, quite consciously, to create a body of short works that, together, could be construed as a unified whole. Like Emily Dickinson (whom Kerouac admired, and whom he imitates briefly at the close of the "205th Chorus"), Yeats worked to make his poems meaningful both independently and as part of a larger scheme. Also like Dickinson, his early poems were closely bound to the structure of song, and his mature work represents, in part, the attempt to move away from such rigid forms toward a method of composition that facilitated the discovery of form. The effect of Yeats's labors is that the body of his poetry became an extended narrative with beginning, middle, and end periods.

In contemporary American poetry, one work stands out as an obvious parallel to *Mexico City Blues*: John Berryman's *Dream Songs*. Berryman, a Confessional poet, began his extended poem in 1955, the same year the Johnson edition of Emily Dickinson's poems appeared and the year in which Kerouac composed *Mexico City Blues*. Though their methods of composition differed radically—Kerouac completing his work in just a few months and Berryman prolonging his for many years—the form of their poems is remarkably similar. Like Kerouac, Berryman limited the size of his poems severely, in imitation of the sonnet. His fifteen lines is equivalent to Kerouac's single notebook page, though technically it may seem more respectable. Through repetition both poems combine this limited lyric form with an overarching narrative. Both poems contain a strong surreal element and a good deal of autobiography and make use of an interlocutor to provide some dramatic tension. And obviously both use a musical metaphor for their organization. Apparently Berryman's poem revolutionized the work of his friend Robert Lowell and thus transformed Confessional poetry from a potentially convoluted self-referential discourse into a more direct and dramatic poetry of statement. Likewise, Kerouac, as Michael McClure has testified, transformed the work of his friends in the avant-garde. Here, the mainstream and the experimental mirror one another.

The distinction Kerouac makes in *Big Sur* between his poetry of "language spinning" and McClure's poetry of ideas may not be the crucial distinction in apprehending the form of *Mexico City Blues*, but it does indicate once again the dialectical nature of his poetics. Kerouac thought himself at odds with the literary establishment, at odds with the work of his own contemporaries in the avant-garde, and at odds with conflicting tendencies within himself. Yet he intuitively grasped in the literary tradition a formal dialectic that could transmute his personal conflicts into poetic tension. This is the function of his combination of lyric and narrative, cumulation and repetition, language spinning and ideas, in a metaphorically musical structure. His tight restrictions on the length of individual choruses in *Mexico City Blues* demanded the economy of diction favored by the Imagists, while the repetitive structure and the metaphor of improvisation provided him with a fluid form for a long poem.

Clark has found evidence of a similar dialectic in Kerouac's prose in the quest for what Kerouac called "deep form." In 1951, the biographer says, about the time of the composition of the scroll version of *On the Road*, Kerouac decided that his prose method

> had separated into two divergent currents: one moving toward a subjective, lyrical vision—the "metaphysical" strain in his *Dr. Sax* notes and in the "vertical" portrait work in Neal's childhood; the other toward a more historical, external perspective— as in the April *Road* with its speedy "horizontal narrative." (97)

Yet Clark also notes that at this time: " 'Deep form'—a resolution of both metaphysical vertical depth and horizontal narrative movement—still obsessed and eluded him" (98). One way to understand the form of *Mexico City Blues* is to see it as the fulfillment of Kerouac's search for "deep form," for a form that would express both image and sound, depth and breadth, thought and action, time and space. At the same time, the poem satisfies the continuing demand in Western poetry for a form that combines lyric and narrative, and in effect, it allows Kerouac both to spin language and to present ideas. In this formal sense, then, *Mexico City Blues* marks the climax of Kerouac's career.

Kerouac considered himself an explorer of form, and the form he contrived for *Mexico City Blues* has both poetic and metaphysical significance. "Mastering older poetic forms was 'child's play,' Kerouac asserted, compared to the task of writing an American poetry with a 'Buddhist base,' which was the only fresh and true direction he saw for it" (Nicosia 475). His Buddhist studies, in turn, led Kerouac to the realization that "the phenomenon of form is inadequate to incarnate Buddhahood," and he recognized that "it can only serve as a mere expression, a hint of that which is inconceivable" (Goddard 103). The Buddhist content of the poem challenged Kerouac to find a comparable form, one that dispelled the illusion of its own permanence. Nicosia provides many enlightening insights into this aspect of the poem's form. "The process of writing the poem," he says, "has become the poem's subject" (481), and he notes elsewhere that Kerouac once reminded Lawrence Ferlinghetti "that poetry was more a quality than a form" (565).

Kerouac's awareness of the insubstantiality of form caused him to value highly—perhaps to overvalue—the sounds of words. "Kerouac retreats from meaning," Nicosia explains, "into the direct communication of rhythm and harmonies of sound" (459). This retreat may account for his description of himself as a "language spinner." According to Nicosia, Kerouac took the Romantic and Modernist insistence on the spoken value of poetic language one step farther to "the apprehension that rhythm develops within the thought process rather than being created by thought" (453) so that, in reducing *Mexico City Blues* to its primary value as sound, he felt he was getting in touch with the wellspring of poetry and of consciousness itself. Through his development of stream of consciousness, he tries to merge the thought processes with his description of them, and the result is a focus on speech production. Not only did he love to try to record the sounds that surrounded him (Gifford and Lee 63, Nicosia 170, McNally 283), but he also reveled in the act of speaking. In *Mexico City Blues* the listener finds both kinds of sound: the recording of natural and artificial noise and the orality of speech replicated on the page.

"Kerouac's talk," Allen Ginsberg has said, "was like *Mexico City Blues*, basically" (Gifford and Lee 47). Kerouac's orality organized his poem into strings of sounds—melodies and rhythms—and certain vowel sounds (*o* and *oo*) seem to take precedence. This bears a striking resemblance to Kerouac's speech, as Nicosia observes:

> People were always impressed by Kerouac's special love of sound, which was obvious from just the way Kerouac talked. He pronounced his consonants very distinctly, and rolled his vowels—especially *o*'s and *u*'s—sensuously over his large lower lip, making them hum and whine and moan. (305)

The motifs embodied by speech sounds are the primary means of organizing *Mexico City Blues*. When themes and imagery become disjointed in the poem, continuity usually subsists in sound. I believe it was Kerouac's intention to produce a poem in which meaning is not only modulated by sound, as in most poetry, but one in which sound also becomes the foremost vehicle of meaning. *Mexico City Blues* is, finally, a complex tune.

This is not to say that themes and imagery, the mainstays of traditional poetic organization, are not important in *Mexico City Blues*. The poem is susceptible to the same kind of technical analysis as any poem in English except that in Kerouac's writing both themes and images tend toward sound. As McNally says: "Since Kerouac floated on waves of sound, dialect and puns, he tried to create images that surpassed 'words with true instinctive communication'" (145). Like Whitman, Kerouac admired the "barbaric yawp" of pure animal language. One of the real beauties of the poem is the way the singer handles themes as sounds, mixing and merging them as though they were notes from various melodies. This weaving of themes is artful, and it supports the organization of the poem.

Images also play an important part in creating a feeling of unity. A much more traditional image than the central image of the poem, balloons, is light. By watching the interplay of light imagery in the poem, more or less independent of any specific theme, I will show how Kerouac adapts the traditional poetic technique to his own purposes. Here again, however, the visual tends toward the auditory, and in *Mexico City Blues* the sights and sounds are often indistinguishable.

Finally, several more superficial elements of form demand attention in the next section of this chapter. These include the shape and length of the individual choruses, the ways in which choruses are sometimes joined, the anomaly of the three-part "216th Chorus," the presence of several "rest" choruses, and the effect of the two extended "cantos" on the poem as a whole. I will try to touch on as many traditional concerns of explication as possible to demonstrate Kerouac's handiness at using techniques of alliteration, rhyme, and so on. Together, Kerouac's emphasis on sound and his command of the other structural devices of poetry enabled him to create a masterpiece of Postmodern poetry. His mastery is at once mystical and demonstrable.

In the following section I will discuss these issues in reverse order, beginning with the superficial structure of the poem, then tracing the light imagery in the poem, next addressing the handling of themes, and finally returning to home base, the sound of words.

One of the most obvious formal properties of *Mexico City Blues* is Kerouac's free and easy use of the space on the page. There is little regularity about the indentation or spacing in the choruses and virtually no uniformity in length. (The shortest chorus is the "11th"—seven lines—and the longest is the "227th Chorus"—thirty-one lines.) There are noticeable repetitions in typography, however, that seem to serve organizational purposes. The infinite variations on reverse indentation appear to have no systematic purpose other than to please the eye by varying the appearance of the text; however, on numerous occasions the singer stacks words in a column. The "42nd Chorus" provides a programmatic instance of such a stack. The context is a mock-heroic fantasy, a plot from a B-movie that becomes slightly surreal in the telling. The lines in question look like this:

> Upset the silly laws, anger
> the
> hare
> brain
> bird
> of
> wine.

This thin string may be a punning attempt to make concrete the word *harebrain*, but in any case, by manipulating the eye, it conjures up the feeling of plummeting. This physical sensation—like watching a film of a roller coaster ride made from the front car—presents a force to be reckoned with in the act of interpretation. That is, in addition to the meaning and the sounds, the poem employs gestural qualities that must be accounted for in the overall effect of the poem.

Another striking example of a stack occurs in the "201st Chorus," which ends with this series of lines:

> Over their heads is the unbelievable
> unending
> emptiness
> the enormous
> emptiness
> of the skies.

As the weight of these words accumulates in such a stack, this weight gives each of the words, especially the abstractions, more impact. Something about the eye not returning to the far left margin and something about the squareness of the stacked text give it both a shock value and a solidity in the poem.

The "16th Chorus," one of the most innovative in the book, combines the stack with another of Kerouac's favorite typographic devices, the stairstep. In this chorus the reader finds both right- and left-hand stairs. The effect of these is to slow or speed the eye. In the left-hand stairs, one finds the beginning of the next line quickly, while the reverse is true of the right-hand stairs (that is, a series of lines in which each one is indented farther than the one preceding). Consequently, in the "16th Chorus" the plummeting effect of the stack in the first stanza is followed by two left-hand stairs, which speed the music immensely. The third stanza, however, which consists entirely of a four-line right-hand stair, puts on the brakes and brings the chorus to a rapid—though not abrupt—halt. This seems all the more appropriate because this is the final chorus in a sequence of four.

Another very interesting, though limited, formal phenomenon is a pair of rest choruses, the "11th" and the "138th." Both of these incorporate rather large spaces between the beginning of the last stanza and the end of the stanza preceding. Nicosia characterizes the first of these two choruses as "a statement about its [the poem's] failure to get started" (481). My difficulty with this interpretation is that in the other rest chorus, the singer blanks out, whether from the effects of opium described in the second stanza or from his meditations on the Buddhist doctrine of no-self. Here, in the earlier chorus, the musician is "brooding," literally hatching the form of the rest of the poem. The first ten choruses are dense with the promise of themes to be developed, testimony that rather than difficulty in getting started, the singer has raised such a wealth of themes that his sideman finds it momentarily bewildering. He must catch his breath after the burst that began the music, develop his artistic strategy, and choose a single theme to develop in the next few choruses. The placement of these two choruses indicates that the second of the pair may announce a reordering or new beginning for the latter half of the poem. This second beginning is made in the Buddhist terms of the concept of the annihilation of the self.

Aside from the sheer mystery of the exact number of choruses (ostensibly 242, but really 244), nothing about the structure of *Mexico City Blues* is initially more perplexing than the anomaly of the three-part "216th Chorus." The total number of choruses given in the title of the book is a number divisible into whole numbers only by 1, 2, and itself. This suggests that the structure of the poem is either unitary or two-part. The real number of choruses, counting the three parts of the "216th Chorus" separately, is divisible also by four, suggesting perhaps that the poem may break into four sections.

The function of the "216th Chorus," besides adding two hidden choruses to the total, is somewhat less obscure. It follows closely the "209th Chorus," which announces the finale, and precedes three other choruses (the "217th," "223rd," and "226th") that also sound notes of conclusion. Each of the three parts of the "216th Chorus" serves as the summation of one important theme in the poem. The "A" part clearly marks the culmination of the poem as poem, the "B" part sums up the Buddhist theme of arbitrary conceptions, and the "C" part concludes the autobiographical theme. This three-part culmination, besides being formally unpredicted, reorganizes the priority of the themes in the poem and provides more new linkages between them. In the first part the singer inscribes his signature into the text: "Jean Louis Miseree." The second part is obviously a prayer for strength to complete his newfound mission as a modern bodhisattva. In the third part, the singer images a pastoral existence based on the needs he has discovered in his meditations on his past and in his attempt to apply his study of Buddhism to his life. Art, religion, and life form the triad of Kerouac's commitments.

Given the presence of such elementary structural properties, the continuity of *Mexico City Blues* becomes even more visible in simple linkages of two or more choruses in terms of diction or theme. These linkages begin early in the poem, and by the end the observant reader/listener counts on them as a means of propulsion. The "13th" through "16th" choruses, for instance, are joined first by the theme of Aztec human sacrifice. Then the "15th Chorus" ostensibly presents an interpretation of the two previous choruses. It begins with the word "Meaning." The following chorus also contains the same word in the first line, suggesting that it too interprets what came before. This serial self-interpretation gives the reader an immediate sense of the accumulation of meaning. Just a bit farther on, in the "21st" and "22nd" choruses the singer makes the link with a simple repetition and variation. "Saved my Bhik-kucitas" at the end of the "21st Chorus" becomes "saved my bhik-kucitos" at the beginning of the "22nd Chorus." These connections fulfill the promise of the poem's epigraph, which states that the ideas "sometimes roll from chorus to chorus or from halfway through a chorus to halfway into the next."

The subtle variation of the last line of the chorus in the first line of a following chorus seems to be the singer's preferred mode of joining. In the "130th Chorus," for example, the repeated phrase "where I am" builds to the conclusion "where I am Mild," calling up the theme of compassion in the poem. The first line of the "131st Chorus," however, shifts the phrase to "Where I aim / And do not Miss," suggesting a much more assertive role for the singer. Likewise, the "169th" and "170th" choruses shift "rest in Time" to "rest in Delicacy." These variations are very much like jazz variations on a melody. They have the same effect on the mind that melodic inversions have on the ear. In fact, in the very next pair of choruses, after playing on the phrase "serenade in blue," the singer actually improvises a little scat riff in the second stanza of the "170th Chorus." He then picks this up to begin the second stanza of the following chorus. This comes at a point in the poem where meaning is clearly breaking down into music for the finale.

Another entire order of linkage—much more extended than what I have just discussed—can be found in what I call the "cantos" of *Mexico City Blues*. The first of these, the Lowell Canto (the "87th" through "104th" choruses), involves Kerouac's childhood and dominates the first half of the poem. The second, the Essence of Existence Canto (the "182nd" through "205th" choruses), commands the latter half. These cantos constitute the dual climax of the poem. There is another extended set of choruses that might be called the Garver Canto, but because these choruses are so widely dispersed throughout the poem, I hesitate to give them the same designation. Nevertheless, they might comprise a sort of "floating canto," focused in such places as the "33rd" to "40th," the "52nd" to "59th," the "70th" to "80th," and the "162nd" to "166th" choruses. In fact, the number of choruses devoted in whole or part to Garver—thirty-eight by my count—exceeds the number in either of the other cantos, even if the outriding autobiographical choruses (about 15 in number) are included in the Lowell Canto. The poem is deceptive in this respect, and it is difficult to determine the exact status of the singer's interlocutor because of the indeterminacy of the Garver Canto. He may be muse, or he may be metaphor.

The Lowell Canto, on the other hand, is clearly one of the focal points of the poem. The autobiographical reference, in formal terms, is largely restricted to the first half of *Mexico City Blues*. Only eight substantial autobiographical allusions can be found after the Lowell Canto (in the "124th," "146th," "149th," "160th," "179th," "187th," "204th," and "213th" choruses), suggesting that Kerouac's resolve to reinterpret his early life in Buddhist terms is successful. Autobiography gives way almost entirely to theological speculation in the second half of the poem. That speculation climaxes in the Essence of Existence Canto, the twenty-three choruses beginning with the "182nd." Within this section (the "194th" through "197th" choruses), Nicosia places the "crisis" of the poem (485), which he takes to be "a major turning away from Buddhism" in the "197th Chorus" (487).

Despite the soundness of his judgment in almost every other respect, I think Nicosia has misperceived the meaning here. What actually happens is not a turning away from Buddhism but a turning away from the dependence on the terminology of Buddhism. As a matter of fact, this is a mark of enlightenment, not a rejection. The singer has simply achieved the realization that the words that describe the doctrine are empty, arbitrary conceptions. His task from this point forward is to practice his Buddhism rather than to speculate about it. In this sense, the Essence of Existence Canto marks the great resolution of conflict in the poem. Suffering still remains, but ego has been neutralized. The singing continues, but the singer is no longer attached to his song. He has come within earshot of the transcendental silence.

Besides autobiography and Buddhism, many other themes connect the choruses of *Mexico City Blues*, although they are not organized into cantos. Sometimes they consist simply of repeated words. The careful reader/listener of the poem will eventually find a concatenation that is almost mind-boggling. My annotations show that almost every chorus is connected to another—often many others—by repeated allusions of various kinds. The issues of sin, death, and salvation come to mind. The names of literary figures and jazz musicians form arabesques of meaning. Kerouac conducts allusive discussions of marriage and money, paternity and prayer, romance and fame. The poem is indeed a kind of guidebook to the concerns of his writing, a microcosm of the Duluoz Legend.

Often these themes are borne in or supplemented by images, although some images, such as the rose, seem to stand independent of any theme. In the "3rd Chorus" the singer sets for himself the task of describing his own experience clearly. He will create images in the sense in which we think of them in Modern poetry—Imagism. He refuses to beautify his images, as he avows in the paired "151st" and "152nd" choruses. He chooses "real life not / still life." When he is ready to wind up the poem, he says, "I'm tired of this imagery" ("216th-A Chorus"), and proceeds to give it up. Since I have spent several chapters discussing themes in great detail, and because I have an interest in showing how Kerouac handled more traditional methods of poetic organization, I want to turn briefly to the development of an important traditional image in *Mexico City Blues*, the image of light.

Light—including the sun, moon, and stars—plays a significant part in more than a fourth of the choruses in the poem. It is the most complex and difficult imagery in the poem. It begins in

the very first chorus and culminates in a repetition of that first in-
stance in the "232nd Chorus." It pervades the central themes of
the poem, especially autobiography and Buddhism, and adds a cir-
cadian sense to the momentary concerns of the singer. In sum,
light and its handling provide an index to the traditional means of
organization in *Mexico City Blues*.

Most of the first half of the poem seems to oscillate between
light and darkness, but very quickly one gets the sense that this
polarization has a metaphysical content. The moonlight belongs to
the Buddha ("6th Chorus"), and the Tathagata is both "The
Maker of Light" and "The Destroyer of Light" ("7th Chorus").
Immediately the singer's handling of light imagery takes on the di-
mension of a spiritual struggle. The purpose of this Zoroastrian
battle, however, is not only that light should prevail, as it does,
but that the perceiver of light come to realize *its* identity with
darkness. In the midst of "Lakes of Light" ("8th Chorus"), the
singer must go

> inward
> down
> to
> moon.   ("16th Chorus")

Here, he finds

> Shining essences
> of universes of stars
> disseminated into powder
> and dust —
>   blazing
>   in the dynamo
>   of our thoughts
>   in the forge
>   of the moon.

In this vast interior darkness he apprehends the ultimate nature of
existence: "A bubble pop, a foam snit / in the immensities of the
sea / at midnight in the dark" ("24th Chorus"). This utter dark-

ness is contrasted in the very next chorus to the "bright blankness" indicated by the word "essence." Essence, though it is neither dark nor light, the singer predicts, will finally reveal itself like Dante's vision in the *Paradiso*:

> When we look into the God face
> We see radiant irradiation
> From middleless center
> Of Objectless fire roe-ing
> In a fieldstar all its own.

This is the singer's brilliant destination in the poem, cast in the diction of Gerard Manley Hopkins.

In the next thirty-odd choruses, he explores images of both light and darkness, perhaps symbolizing his concurrent outward and inward journeys. "Tender is the Night" ("30th Chorus"), "Lemon Light" ("31st Chorus"), grape stars ("32nd Chorus"), and daybreak ("37th Chorus") all succeed one another rapidly. In the lovely "66th Chorus," which begins with a line repeated with important variation at the close of the Lowell Canto—"I'd rather die than be famous"—Kerouac combines images of day and night and concludes by foreshadowing the last chorus of the poem. In the first stanza he imagines himself a hermit in the desert by a campfire. In the second stanza it is high noon. In the third stanza it is night, and the singer is able to hear the "zing of silence." This night scene calls up an image from the Diamond Sutra of Buddha discoursing to his disciples around a campfire in the evening. And this, in turn, leads him to the preliminary conclusion that the essence of existence is "Blank / bright" ("66th Chorus").

The prelude to the Lowell Canto is set to the tune of "Harvest Moon," with all its saccharine romance. It is as though Kerouac were replaying the courtship between his parents that brought him into being. His own story, the autobiographical canto itself, begins with "New / Haven Railroads of the Night" ("87th Chorus"), and this same chorus concludes with an antiromantic characterization of his second marriage. The rest of the canto, unlike the chiaroscuro that precedes it, is rich in the colors of daylight. My sense of this is that color itself signified for Kerouac the impressions of discriminating mind, and that the true seeker must reach beyond the illusion of color toward the pure polarities of light and dark, and even beyond them to the light that suffuses the darkness. The "89th Chorus" paints a vivid description of the colorful horrors of life, beginning with the "gray / Immense morning" Kerouac was conceived, proceeding through the "red gory afternoon" of his birth, and concluding with phantoms and howling winds in the "Moony / and Loony nights."

The remainder of the canto draws from a rich—almost raw—palette to paint its scenes. The "Sun of Sadness" shines through the windows of childhood ("92nd Chorus") while the "brown light" Kerouac associated with his childhood homes ("93rd Chorus") contrasts with the "downtown red" of his father's workaday world ("99th Chorus"). These colors are nicely resolved in the "103rd Chorus," which begins with this striking description:

> My father in downtown red
> Walked around like a shadow
> Of ink black, with hat, nodding,
> In the immemorial lights of my dreams.

Kerouac's father, a printer by trade, becomes to his imagination nothing more than a silhouette. The colors are beginning to fade from his memory, partly because of age, partly because of effort to see through them to the source of light. The chorus concludes:

> My remembrance of my father
>   in downtown Lowell
>   walking like cardboard cut
>   across the lost lights
> is the same empty material
> as my father in the grave.

Following the Lowell Canto, the singer senses things "Getting dimmer and dimmer / to the feel" ("122nd Chorus"). His perception of a "Golden Age / of Silent Darkness" in his heart gives a clue to the coming resolution of the imagery and introduces an extended exploration of the darkness. With the exception of one chorus ("123rd") that provides a glimpse of the "blinding light" behind the gloom, and one ("127th"), set in a previous incarnation, that recalls—like Wordsworth's ode—the forgotten knowledge that "white while joyous / was also / Center of lake of light," the middle choruses contain only images of night. The singer finds something universal in the night, opposed to the particulars of daylight, and once again he anticipates the conclusion of the poem when he perceives: "The Blazing Silence in the Night" ("146th Chorus"). Amid "a starry disaster" he hears street children call out the name of a companion, Luz—light ("161st Chorus"). Gradually, out of this earthly darkness, the eternal light returns.

At the outset of the Essence of Existence Canto, the singer comes to the realization that his fears about death are "really radiant / right eternities" ("184th Chorus"). In the course of the canto, this realization rises to a dazzling climax of light imagery. The singer quotes Shinran's phrase about "Clouds of Light" ("191st") and visions of the "Diamond Irradiation" and "waving whitenesses" come to him. Even within he sees "caves of light" ("199th"), and the inward journey yields up the paradox of "white light of black eternity." All this leads to the climactic "200th Chorus," with its "White figures throughout / made of light" and its consummately Postmodern image of the semitrailer in the night as "a square / mass of shining light bars." These images of light, the singer discovers, figure the "empty Apparitional secret / figure of the mind." At the same time he achieves the "One Shiningness" he recognizes that "darkness nullifies / the color / Into Nirvana No." Both the dazzling whiteness and the darkness shaped by lights—the "light bars"—share the same essence.

The metaphysical implications of the light imagery in *Mexico City Blues* are set forth in the "105th Chorus" in a crucial discussion of the nature of reality. Two stanzas carry the gist of it:

Essence is what sunlight is
At the same time that moonlight is,
Both have light, both have shape,
Both have darkness, both are late:

Both are late because empty thereof,
Empty is light, empty is dark,
    what's difference between emptiness
    of brightness and dark?

The singer expands this discussion two choruses later, but the purport of it is clear here. Light in spiritual matters, as in the poem, is a metaphor. Unless and until the seeker recognizes the metaphoric nature of light, he or she will necessarily fail to realize the essential unity of light and darkness, or in other words, the identity between enlightenment and nonenlightenment. As the singer states in the "191st Chorus," the starting place and the goal are one. The means of the journey lies in the "songs that erupt," the "gist of poesy," which "come by themselves . . . stark as prisoners in a cave / Let out to sunlight" ("195th Chorus). It is poetry, at last, that leads to the awareness of essential unity.

Kerouac articulates this unity in the light imagery of *Mexico City Blues*, and just as the poetics give substance to his spiritual quest, his enlightenment provides unity for the poem. The intuition, in the "1st Chorus," that his experience is "All one light" leads him to try to

    describe, self-descried
    in one essential
     l i g h t ,
    the holy gold so-called.   ("177th Chorus")

Finally, in the "232nd Chorus," he has passed "into Change's Lightless Domain," where he is

    Waiting in anticipatory halls
    Of Bar-Light, ranging, searchlights
    Of the Eye, Maitreya and his love,
    The dazzling obscure parade
    of elemental diamond phantoms
    And dominos of chance.

These three choruses are the touchstones of the light imagery that spans the entire poem. Their unitary quality, achieved by great spiritual effort, is transferred by great artistic effort into the poem. This quality of achieved spiritual unity, embodied in figures of light and darkness, becomes a hallmark of traditional formal unity in *Mexico City Blues*.

Like Pound, Kerouac was concerned not only with the image, but also with something even more fundamental: the sound of the words that create the image. In an extremely perceptive chorus, the "21st," he ascribes the lack of musicality in Western poetry to an overemphasis on science. In the East, however, he senses the potential for a new musicality. He makes a playful transition from an allusion to his own Catholicism:

> To us listeners
> Of the Holy See
> Saw,
> said,
> Saved.

This alliteration has, for me, a surprisingly profound meaning. Its implication is that one can transform imagery into sound, and that this transformation somehow leads to salvation. My interpretation is confirmed, I believe, in the last stanza of the the "22nd" chorus (which is paired with the "21st"):

> Importunate fool that I was,
> I raved to fight Saviors
> Instead of listening in
> To the light — still a fool.

This stanza apparently represents an epiphany, since it is followed by a list of actual and imaginary choruses that merges with a list of tunes and finally devolves into a display of sound for sound's sake at the conclusion of the "23rd Chorus."

The transformation of theme and image into sound involves, at least for the singer of the poem, a recognition of the distinction between euphonism and euphemism ("45th Chorus"). "One is sonic," the singer intones, "one is human." It is not his desire to prettify life, so he must not succumb to the desire to make his poetry merely a pleasant music. He must listen carefully to the "oral eloquent air" ("50th Chorus"), to the sounds of the sea ("53rd Chorus"), and to "the zing of silence" ("64th Chorus"), in order to confirm that both euphemism and euphonism are "imaginary metaphors" ("45th Chorus"). Ultimately, by pressing his poetry in the direction of sound, the singer hopes to hear the "silence you hear / inside the emptiness" ("67th Chorus"). Just as the distinction between light and darkness proved to be empty, so does the distinction between sound and silence.

In the "73rd Chorus" the singer incants "The Book of Pluviums"—that is, the book of rains or rainsounds, which turns out to be a collage of quotation, cliché, onomatopoeia, and nonsense, not all of it pleasant to the ear. Now he has begun to sing without discriminating among sounds. He hears what he hears without reference to value judgment. Somewhat later, he recognizes in reality "innumeral infinite songs" ("132nd Chorus"). He has successfully converted image into sound, and in the "171st Chorus" he begins to sing his own uninhibited melody. Spontaneity is one way to access these undiscriminating songs, and again, they are the "songs that erupt" ("195th Chorus").

One problem remains that requires a further transformation. The radio, which usually has positive connotations for Kerouac, here also represents the mass replication of discriminated sounds. In the "173rd Chorus" the singer calls it the "Ultimo Actual Soundbody." He must avoid, if possible, becoming a mere conduit, like the radio, for sounds that characterize the essence of existence incorrectly. The singer has placed an appropriate motto earlier in the poem:

> The Tathata
> of
> Eminence
> is
> Silence.   ("141st Chorus")

Now, he takes up its meaning. In the "188th Chorus" he vows to pray to the Buddhist masters "and ask them to let me / hear their transcendental / silence sound" in order to learn to "sing sound silence / of my sound." The singer has transformed vision into voice, and now—against all poetic odds—he must transform voice into silence.

After a bit he wonders if he should be singing "quiet hum-sound" ("199th Chorus"). Directly he discovers, on the model of animal cries, how to open his "mouth to say something empty" ("206th Chorus"). A revelation comes to him in this same chorus: "sound is noise." The solution for his dilemma—how to sing the sound of emptiness—takes the form of a paradox: "Because you cant sing / open yr mouth with poems." The poem, apparently, is a form of utterance capable of uttering its own silence, as in the rest choruses perhaps. As a form of communication, it can point to the sound and point out that it, like the themes and images, is empty. In this way it performs the valuable service of making sound, which is "un-self-enlightenable," accessible as a means of enlightment to human beings. The singer then is helping to prevent sound from "blaring unrecognized / as emptiness and silence."

The "213th Chorus," picking up the nonsense form of "Pull My Daisy," the Ginsberg-Cassady-Kerouac collaboration, begins an object lesson in the use of poetry to point out the emptiness of sound. This continues right through to the "216th-A Chorus," in which the singer concludes his tour de force by putting his signature to the sound. Among other hints of the coming end of the poem, the singer announces in the "223rd Chorus" his "fonally finalles." He has made his point and now resolves to "Sing a little ditty of the moon inside the loony / boon of snow white blooms." At the last, here, the light images are contained within his ditty, a microcosm of the poem as a whole. This little song leads to the singer's final renunciation of his medium. He sings in the "242nd Chorus":

> The sound in your mind
> is the first sound
>   that you could sing
>
> If you were singing
> at a cash register
>   with nothing on yr mind —.

Nicosia confirms that the singer has reached his goal. "The final, 242nd Chorus," he says, "begins with an account of the 'Diamond Samadhi,' the experience of hearing the hush of soundlessness, which is supposed to illustrate the Buddhist truth that existence is mind created" (489).

Kerouac's spiritual quest propelled him past the ordinary traditional methods of poetic organization. The frankness and seriousness of his endeavor led him to a form beyond the mechanics of typography, past the efficacy of images, outside the very boundaries of sound. *Mexico City Blues*, at last, resolves itself into a special silence, a silence that recalls to us that the poet's medium is just a finger pointing in the right direction. As a result of his mastery of poetic organization, Kerouac becomes, in my view, what he calls Charlie Parker in his poem: a "great musician and a great / creator of forms" ("239th Chorus"). Like Bird, Kerouac transcends even art and enters into the realm of pure actuality.

9

Conclusion

Let a man be either a hero or a saint.
In between lies, not wisdom, but banality.

Included in Book One of *Dr. Sax*, the novel Kerouac intended to be an extension of the Faust legend, is a small map of the Lowell neighborhood called Pawtucketville, where Kerouac lived the years of his early adolescence. The map shows Phebe Street, where the character Jackie Duluoz lived in a house facing that of his friend G.J.; Phebe Street came to a dead end on Sarah Street at a park that was inhabited by ghosts. Gershom ran along one side of the park, Riverside along the other. Either street provided a safe route home for the boys, who "never walked home across the field, instead went Riverside-Sarah or Gershom-Sarah, Phebe . . . was the center of two prongs" (*Dr. Sax* 42). I believe those two prongs represent two opposing qualities of language, two ways of getting home, and Kerouac's map of his boyhood aptly represents my map of the achievement of his poetry. Both routes lead to the same destination.

In *Word Cultures* Robin Lydenberg has argued brilliantly about William S. Burroughs's use of language. To translate her argument into my terms, it seems that Burroughs has adopted a neither/nor approach. He refuses to allow the reader to allegorize his texts, yet he never forces his texts beyond signification. Kerouac, his informal student and former collaborator, on the other hand, takes what might be called a complementary approach: both/and. Unlike Burroughs, Kerouac preferred multiple allegories deployed dialectically. He arrays fiction against poetry, memory against egolessness, society against solitude, sign against sound, Catholicism against Buddhism, control against spontaneity, and narrative against lyric. Further, by means of these contraries, he always manages to force his texts into the realm of pure sound. While Burroughs's method is one of negation, Kerouac's is one of balance. Though it is possible to find the same features of balance at work in Kerouac's fiction, especially the two novels of his early Buddhist period—*Tristessa* and *Visions of Gerard*—*Mexico City Blues* showcases the advantages of his poetics perfectly. He wrote it at a fateful time in his life when his conflicts, like so many governing stars, had come into auspicious alignment.

Kerouac's thinking, like that of most Westerners, was profoundly dualistic. His singular advantage lay in his art, which, far from disguising the polarities of his life, builds them into its own music for all to hear. In Kerouac's complex counterpoint, his listeners may find a source of wonder that the divisions of our consciousness do not always lead to such balance. Kerouac's life, by contrast, proves with certainty that these divisions do indeed disable and destroy. The mystery of art, as *Mexico City Blues* so amply illustrates, is that it transforms life without falsifying it. The process is quite alchemical. It transmutes the material conditions of existence, which run to extremes of pain and pleasure, into a set of ideal conditions that are optimally organized to create a sense of equilibrium. Through this equilibrium the mind renews its thoughts and feelings by exploring the new territory opened in the space between the contraries and pursues inwardly its goal of self-discovery. As the poet Kerouac says in the "225th Chorus,"

Yet I keep restless mental searching
And geographical meandering
To find the Holy Inside Milk
Damema gave to all.

Despite the homage so many writers have paid to Jack Kerouac, his value is still underestimated. Not only did he alter the face of American popular culture with his fiction, but he has also helped determine the future of American poetry by providing our tradition with one of its most original long poems. Among his other contributions, he appears to me to be one of the great religious writers of our time. In the years to come, Jack Kerouac's stature will undoubtedly grow, despite the reactionary criticism that has tried to belittle his contributions to literature by confusing his work with his lifestyle. Once the extent of his grasp of literary tradition has been fully explored, it will be impossible to deny him the status for which he ardently longed: the sainthood of literary canonization.

I hope to have contributed solid testimony to the mastery of his art, and I believe that this *Map* will help guide others—especially the cynics—to a realization of the lasting quality of Kerouac's insight: his uncanny ability to fuse the colloquial with the literary. His was at heart a Romantic project, but even in a time of rapid and sweeping changes in the canon, *Mexico City Blues* clearly satisfies Whitman's demand for a truly comprehensive democratic literature. The poem is, as Michael McClure affirms in *Scratching the Beat Surface*, Kerouac's "masterpiece": "a religious poem startling in its majesty and comedy and gentleness and vision" (71).

Works Cited and Consulted
General Index
Index to Choruses

Works Cited and Consulted

Amram, David. *Vibrations: The Adventures and Musical Times of David Amram.* New York: MacMillan, 1968.

Asvaghosa. *Buddhacarita; or, Acts of the Buddha.* Ed. E. H. Johnson. New Delhi: Oriental Books Reprint, 1972.

Baraka, Amiri. *The Autobiography of LeRoi Jones.* New York: Freundlich, 1984.

————. *Blues People: The Negro Experience in White America and Music That Developed from It.* New York: Morrow, 1963.

————, ed. *The Moderns.* New York: Corinth, 1963.

Berrigan, Ted. "The Art of Fiction XLI: Jack Kerouac." *The Paris Review* 43 (1968): 60–105.

Burroughs, William S. *Junky.* New York: Viking Penguin, 1977.

————. *Queer.* New York: Viking Penguin, 1985.

Charters, Ann. *Kerouac: A Biography.* New York: St. Martins, 1987.

Clark, Tom. *Jack Kerouac.* New York: Harcourt, 1984.

Fields, Rick. *How the Swans Came to the Lake: A Narrative History of Buddhism in America.* Boulder: Shambala, 1981.

Foucault, Michel. *Madness and Civilization: A History of Insanity in the Age of Reason.* New York: Random, 1988.

Garon, Paul. *Blues and the Poetic Spirit.* New York: Da Capo, 1975.

Gifford, Barry, and Lawrence Lee. *Jack's Book: An Oral Biography of Jack Kerouac.* New York: Penguin-NAL, 1979.

Ginsberg, Allen. *Collected Poems 1947-1980.* New York: Harper, 1984.

————. *Howl and Other Poems.* San Francisco: City Lights, 1956.

Goddard, Dwight, ed. *A Buddhist Bible.* Boston: Beacon, 1970.

Gunn, Drewey Wayne. *American and British Writers in Mexico, 1556–1973.* Austin: U of Texas P, 1969.

Hipkiss, Robert A. *Jack Kerouac: Prophet of the New Romanticism.* Lawrence, KS: Regents Press, 1976.

Jung, C. G. "On the Nature of the Psyche." *The Basic Writings of C. G. Jung.* Ed. Violet Straub de Laszlo. New York: Modern Library, 1959. 37–104.

Kerouac, Jack. *Big Sur.* New York: McGraw, 1981.

———. *Book of Dreams.* San Francisco: City Lights, 1961.

———. *Desolation Angels.* New York: Putnam's, 1980.

———. *Dr. Sax: Faust Part Three.* New York: Grove, 1975.

———. *Heaven & Other Poems.* Ed. Don Allen. San Francisco: Grey Fox, 1977.

———. *Lonesome Traveler.* New York: Grove, 1960.

———. *Maggie Cassidy.* New York: McGraw, 1978.

———. *Mexico City Blues (242 Choruses).* New York: Grove, 1959.

———. *On the Road.* Ed. Scott Donaldson. New York: Penguin-NAL, 1985.

———. *Satori in Paris.* New York: Grove, 1966.

———. *Scattered Poems.* Comp. Ann Charters. San Francisco: City Lights, 1971.

———. *The Scripture of the Golden Eternity.* New York: Totem/Corinth, 1970.

———. *The Subterraneans.* New York: Grove, 1981.

———. *The Town and the City.* New York: Harcourt, 1983.

———. *Trip Trap.* With Albert Saijo and Lew Welch. Bolinas, CA: Grey Fox, 1973.

———. *Tristessa.* New York: McGraw, 1978.

———. *Vanity of Duluoz: An Adventurous Education, 1935–46.* London: Quartet, 1975.

———. *Visions of Cody.* New York: McGraw, 1974.

———. *Visions of Gerard.* New York: McGraw, 1976.

Kerouac, Jan. *Baby Driver.* New York: Holt, 1983.

———. *Trainsong.* New York: Holt, 1988.

Kesey, Ken. *Demon Box.* New York: Viking Penguin, 1986.

———. *Kesey's Garage Sale.* New York: Viking, 1973.

Kristeva, Julia. *The Kristeva Reader.* New York: Columbia UP, 1986.

Lydenberg, Robin. *Word Cultures: Radical Theory and Practice in William S. Burroughs' Fiction.* Urbana: U of Illinois P, 1987.

McClure, Michael. *Scratching the Beat Surface.* San Francisco: North Point, 1982.

McDarrah, Fred. *Kerouac and Friends: A Beat Generation Album.* New York: Morrow, 1984.

McNally, Dennis. *Desolate Angel: Jack Kerouac, the Beat Generation, and America.* New York: Random, 1979.

Mottram, Eric. Introduction. *The Scripture of the Golden Eternity.* By Jack Kerouac. New York: Totem/Corinth, 1970.

Nicosia, Gerald. *Memory Babe: A Critical Biography of Jack Kerouac.* New York: Grove, 1983.

Perkins, David. *Wordsworth and the Poetry of Sincerity.* Cambridge: Harvard UP, 1964.

Pound, Ezra. *ABC of Reading.* New York: New Direction, 1987.

Reisner, Robert, ed. *Bird: The Legend of Charlie Parker.* New York: Da Capo, 1977.

Sorrell, Richard. "The Catholicism of Jack Kerouac." *Studies in Religion* 11 (1982): 189–200.

Spengler, Oswald. *The Decline of the West.* Trans. Charles Francis Atkinson. New York: Knopf, 1926.

Tallman, Warren. "Kerouac's Sound." *A Casebook on the Beat.* Ed. Thomas Parkinson. New York: Crowell, 1961. 215–29.

Tytell, John. *Naked Angels: The Lives and Literature of the Beat Generation.* New York: Grove, 1976.

Watts, Alan. "Beat Zen, Square Zen, and Zen." *Chicago Review* 12 (1958): 3–11.

Weinreich, Regina. *The Spontaneous Poetics of Jack Kerouac: A Study of the Fiction.* Carbondale: Southern Illinois UP, 1987.

Wolfe, Tom. *The Electric Kool-Aid Acid Test.* New York: Bantam, 1968.

General Index

Index of Choruses

James T. Jones was born and raised in Decatur, Illinois, where he attended Catholic schools. He earned his B.A. and M.A. degrees in English at Eastern Illinois University in Charleston, Illinois. He earned his Ph.D. in modern American literature in 1980 at Southern Illinois University at Carbondale, where he held a special doctoral assistantship. His first book, *Wayward Skeptic: The Theories of R. P. Blackmur*, was published by the University of Illinois Press in 1986. He has also edited *Outsider at the Heart of Things: Essays of R. P. Blackmur*, published by the University of Illinois Press in 1989. Though he maintains an active interest in the history of New Criticism, he is currently at work on a book-length study of Jack Kerouac's fiction. Since 1983 Jones has taught nineteenth- and twentieth-century American literature at Southwest Missouri State University.